Beginning

JAZZ DANCE

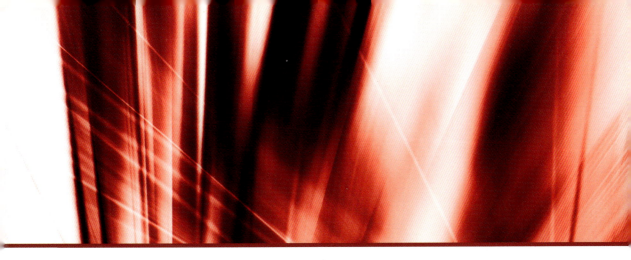

Beginning
JAZZ DANCE

INTERACTIVE DANCE SERIES

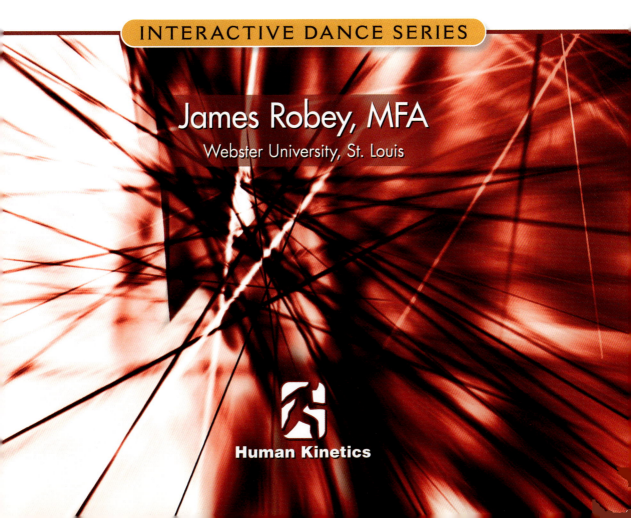

James Robey, MFA
Webster University, St. Louis

Human Kinetics

Library of Congress Cataloging-in-Publication Data

Robey, James, 1971-

Beginning jazz dance / James Robey, Webster University.

   pages cm

Includes bibliographical references and index.

1. Jazz dance. I. Title.

GV1753.R64 2015

793.3'3--dc23

                        2015008672

ISBN: 978-1-4504-6894-7 (print)

The web addresses cited in this text were current as of July 2015, unless otherwise noted.

Acquisitions Editor: Gayle Kassing, PhD; **Developmental Editor:** Bethany J. Bentley; **Managing Editor:** Anne E. Mrozek; **Copyeditor:** Bob Replinger; **Indexer:** Dan Connolly; **Permissions Manager:** Dalene Reeder; **Graphic Designer:** Joe Buck; **Cover Designer:** Keith Blomberg; **Photographer (cover):** Bernard Wolff; photographs © Human Kinetics; **Photographer (interior):** Bernard Wolff; photographs © Human Kinetics, unless otherwise noted; photos on pages 132, 134, 137, 138, and 143 © Photofest; **Photo Asset Manager:** Laura Fitch; **Visual Production Assistant:** Joyce Brumfield; **Photo Production Manager:** Jason Allen; **Art Manager:** Kelly Hendren; **Associate Art Manager:** Alan L. Wilborn; **Illustrations**: © Human Kinetics, unless otherwise noted; **Printer:** Versa Press

We thank Webster University in St. Louis, Missouri, for assistance in providing the location for the photo shoot for this book.

The video contents of this product are licensed for educational public performance for viewing by a traditional (live) audience, via closed circuit television, or via computerized local area networks within a single building or geographically unified campus. To request a license to broadcast these contents to a wider audience—for example, throughout a school district or state, or on a television station—please contact your sales representative (www.HumanKinetics.com/SalesRepresentatives).

Printed in the United States of America

10 9 8 7 6 5 4 3 2 1

Human Kinetics
Website: www.HumanKinetics.com

United States: Human Kinetics
P.O. Box 5076
Champaign, IL 61825-5076
800-747-4457
e-mail: humank@hkusa.com

Canada: Human Kinetics
475 Devonshire Road Unit 100
Windsor, ON N8Y 2L5
800-465-7301 (in Canada only)
e-mail: info@hkcanada.com

Europe: Human Kinetics
107 Bradford Road
Stanningley
Leeds LS28 6AT, United Kingdom
+44 (0) 113 255 5665
e-mail: hk@hkeurope.com

Australia: Human Kinetics
57A Price Avenue
Lower Mitcham, South Australia 5062
08 8372 0999
e-mail: info@hkaustralia.com

New Zealand: Human Kinetics
P.O. Box 80
Mitcham Shopping Centre, South Australia 5062
0800 222 062
e-mail: info@hknewzealand.com

E6165

Contents

Preface   vii
Acknowledgments   ix
How to Use the Web Resource   xi

1 Introduction to Jazz Dance   1

Defining Jazz Dance 2
Benefits of Studying Jazz Dance. 6
Jazz Dance Class Expectations and Etiquette 7
Summary. 9

2 Preparing for Class   11

Dressing for Class 12
Carrying Dance Gear 13
Preparing Yourself Mentally and Physically 14
Jazz Dance Class Structure 19
Roles of the Teacher, Musician, and Students 22
Summary. 23

3 Safety and Health   25

Studio Safety 26
Personal Safety. 27
Basic Anatomy and Kinesiology. 28
Preventing and Treating Common Jazz Dance Injuries 31
Nutrition, Hydration, and Rest 35
Summary. 36

4 Learning and Performing Jazz Dance Technique   37

Learning Movement Technique. 38
Analyzing Movement Skills 40
Honing Musicality and Rhythmic Skills 45
Enhancing Performance in Class. 47
Developing a Performance Attitude 51
Summary. 54

5 Basic Jazz Dance Positions 55

Body Alignment 56
Positions of the Feet 60
Positions of the Arms 62
Hand Positions 70
Positions of the Body 72
Studio and Stage Directions 77
Summary. 78

6 Basic Jazz Dance Techniques 79

Getting Started. 80
Basic Warm-Up Techniques 80
Basic Isolation Techniques. 83
Basic Coordination Techniques .87
Basic Conditioning Techniques. .89
Summary. 94

7 In the Center and Across the Floor 95

Exercises in the Center 96
Exercises Across the Floor 109
Types of Combinations 122
Summary. 123

8 History of Jazz Dance 125

Development of Jazz Dance as a Performing Art 126
Jazz Dance Forms and Styles .142
Viewing Jazz Dance Performances 146
Summary. 149

Glossary   151
References and Resources   155
Index   157
About the Author   163

Preface

The exhilaration of jazz dance with its grooving energy, dynamic rhythms, and infectious music makes jazz dance class an exciting experience. Getting to know the basics of jazz dance helps you get the most of that experience. *Beginning Jazz Dance* provides novice dancers a complete summary of expectations, basic techniques, background information, and step-by-step instructions for success in the jazz dance class. Besides serving as a handbook for beginning students, *Beginning Jazz Dance* also functions as a comprehensive guide for advanced students and jazz dance enthusiasts.

Chapter 1, "Introduction to Jazz Dance," explores the questions "What is jazz dance?" "Why study jazz dance?" and "What are the expectations and rules of class?" By providing a clear definition of jazz dance based on its core elements, explaining the values and benefits of studying jazz dance, and clarifying common class expectations, rules, and etiquette, *Beginning Jazz Dance* starts the student off on the right foot in the study of jazz dance.

Chapter 2, "Preparing for Class," investigates answers to the questions "What should I wear?" "How do I get ready for class?" "What are the roles of the student, teacher, and musician?" and "How is class structured?" By learning about the common structure of jazz dance class, the roles of everyone in the studio, ways to dress, and ways to prepare physically and mentally, jazz dance students will achieve greater success and joy in the studio.

In chapter 3, "Safety and Health," dancers discover general and personal safety issues, injury prevention tips, and healthy nutrition guidelines as a means of support for the physical activity of the jazz dance class. By learning the benefits of a thorough warm-up, proper alignment, and basic anatomy and kinesiology, students gather the information needed for safe and healthy experiences in jazz dance class.

In chapter 4, "Learning and Performing Jazz Dance Technique," students learn what to expect from the learning experience and how to deal with both the excitement of breakthroughs and the frustration presented by inevitable challenges. Students also discover class-taking techniques, getting the most out of feedback, and keys to performance—both in the class and on the stage.

Chapter 5, "Basic Jazz Dance Positions," introduces basic body alignment as well as the basic foot, arm, hand, and body positions used in jazz dance classes. Chapter 6, "Basic Jazz Dance Techniques," provides students with step-by-step instructions for the exercises that commonly begin jazz dance class, including basic warm-up, isolation, coordination, and conditioning techniques.

In chapter 7, "In the Center and Across the Floor," students learn the vocabulary of jazz dance starting with center exercises and leading to locomotor steps across the floor that include jazz walks, kicks (or battements), turns, leaps, and floor work. A discussion of the types of combinations that might be explored at the end of class and the value of a cool-down ritual follows.

Chapter 8, "History of Jazz Dance," presents a summary of the development of jazz dance as an art, important artists and choreographers, significant jazz dance works, and jazz dance forms and styles.

The web resource that accompanies this book offers supplemental interactive instruction, such as video clips of jazz dance techniques, worksheets and assignments, links to further study, and more. Visit www.HumanKinetics.com/BeginningJazzDance to check it out.

Whatever your dance experience, *Beginning Jazz Dance* gives you context and background information that will enhance your understanding of the art form, enabling you to become a knowledgeable, thinking artist. *Beginning Jazz Dance* gives you the chance to turn the infectious energy, rhythms, and dynamics of jazz dance into a lifelong passion.

eBook
available at
your campus bookstore
or HumanKinetics.com

Acknowledgments

First and foremost, I thank my wife and artistic partner Melissa Gerth for her insight, intelligence, and patient support during the process of writing this book. I also thank my son Jakobi for his understanding in all the times my head was buried in this project. Also, thank you to my brother Jason Robey whose athletic training expertise was integral in developing safe and effective exercises for jazz dance.

I thank my first dance teacher Francine LeRoy for teaching me a passion for jazz dance and my college professor Priscilla Wagner for teaching me that jazz dance is a profound art form worthy of deep study and respect.

I extend a special thank you to Howard Turner and the Ridgefield Conservatory of Dance for serving as a proving ground and support system for the ideas and approaches expressed in this book. I also extend a special thank you to Webster University for the support, time, and space to make this project possible. A special thanks goes to my student assistants Lanese Collier, Abby Contreras, DJ Duncan, Claire Francescon, Kevin Hamilton, Jacob Henss, Cheyenne Phillips, and Lauren Sandberg as well as my colleagues Alan Schilling and Beckah Reed.

Finally, the entire Human Kinetics team has been incredible throughout this process. Thank you to Bethany Bentley, Anne Mrozek, and especially to Gayle Kassing for her guidance, wisdom, and encouragement. I truly appreciate all who supported and inspired this book and hope that others will come to appreciate jazz dance as a profound art form through your collective efforts.

How to Use the Web Resource

In a jazz dance class, steps and combinations can occur quickly. They can contain a large number of new movements or small additions to movements you have already learned. But you have an added advantage! Your personal tutor is just a few clicks away and is always available to help you remember and practice the exercises and steps executed in class. You can study between class meetings or when doing mental practice to memorize exercises or movement. Check out the web resource that accompanies the book at www.HumanKinetics.com/BeginningJazzDance.

The web resource is an interactive tool that you can use to enhance your understanding of beginning jazz dance technique, review what you studied in class, or prepare for performance testing. It includes information about each position or movement, including notes for correct performance; photos of foot, arm, and hand positions; and video clips of jazz dance techniques. Also included are interactive quizzes for each chapter of the *Beginning Jazz Dance* text, which let you test your knowledge of concepts, jazz dance basics, terminology, and more.

In a beginning jazz dance class, students learn about jazz technique, jazz dance as an art form, and themselves. The supplementary materials section of the web resource contains the following additional components for each chapter of the *Beginning Jazz Dance* text. These components support both learning in the jazz dance class and exploring more about the world of jazz dance.

- Glossary terms from the text are presented so that you can check your knowledge of the translated meaning of the term as well as a description of the term.
- Web links give you a starting place to learn more about jazz dance techniques, styles, and dance companies.
- Chapters include e-journaling prompts, handouts, and assignments that will help you think more deeply about beginning jazz dance class.
- Other assignments include specific activities to apply concepts and ideas about jazz dance.

This web resource helps you individualize your learning experience so that you can connect to, expand, and apply your learning of beginning jazz dance, enhancing your success and enjoyment in the study of this dance form.

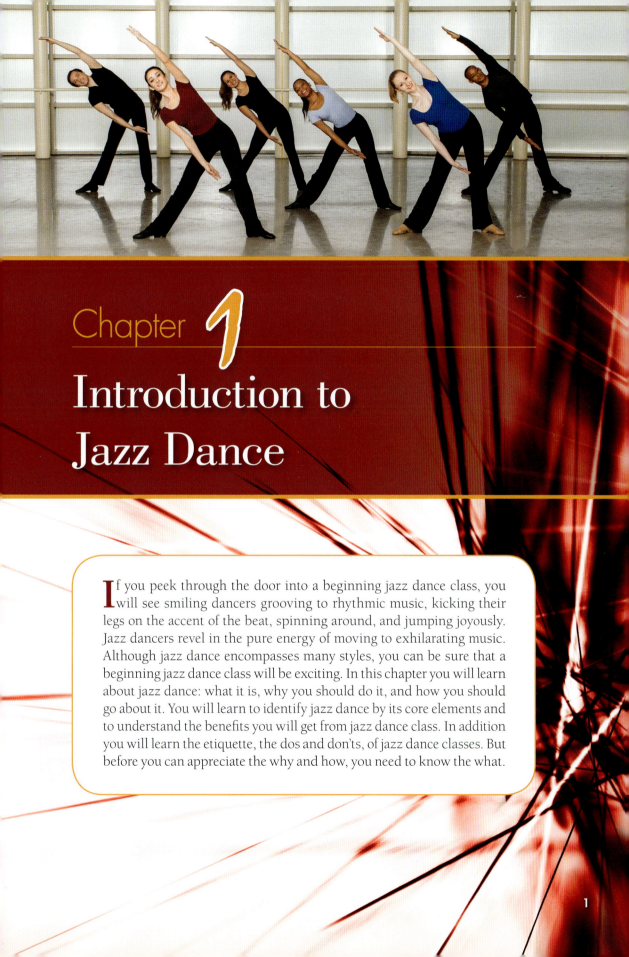

Chapter *1*

Introduction to Jazz Dance

If you peek through the door into a beginning jazz dance class, you will see smiling dancers grooving to rhythmic music, kicking their legs on the accent of the beat, spinning around, and jumping joyously. Jazz dancers revel in the pure energy of moving to exhilarating music. Although jazz dance encompasses many styles, you can be sure that a beginning jazz dance class will be exciting. In this chapter you will learn about jazz dance: what it is, why you should do it, and how you should go about it. You will learn to identify jazz dance by its core elements and to understand the benefits you will get from jazz dance class. In addition you will learn the etiquette, the dos and don'ts, of jazz dance classes. But before you can appreciate the why and how, you need to know the what.

DEFINING JAZZ DANCE

If you asked a dozen jazz dancers what jazz dance is, you might get a dozen different answers. Speaking broadly, jazz dance is a uniquely American art form with roots in West African traditional dance. It is often performed with a rhythmic focus, in dialogue with gravity, with direct expression, and embracing individual style. Jazz dance often appears in Broadway musicals, concert dance companies, movies, television, music videos, Las Vegas shows, commercials, theme parks, and cruise ships.

The relative youth of jazz dance, its variety of styles, and shifts in popular trends make it tough to form a concise definition. Few recognize the link between authentic jazz dance steps such as the Charleston in 1920 and the pyrotechnical switch leap in popular commercial dance today. Even jazz dance experts disagree on the definition of jazz dance. In this book we take the point of view that you cannot define jazz dance simply by its steps; you have to look at its qualities, and to do that, you have to understand how it got its name.

The term *jazz dance* originally applied to the social dancing done to jazz music in the early 1900s. Just as we refer to the dance done to hip-hop music today as hip-hop dancing, the dance done to jazz music in the early 1900s was jazz dancing. Later, social jazz dance steps were integrated with ballet and modern when musical theater choreographers began incorporating social dance into their work.

Because of the variety of jazz dance steps and their nature to evolve and change with the coming and going of trends, defining jazz dance by its steps alone is difficult. Rather, imagine looking at jazz dance as you would a family member. Your brother may not have your mother's or father's ears, but if he has your mother's eyes, your father's chin, and your grandmother's smile, you see the family resemblance. Jazz dance, too, can be looked at for its family resemblance based on a number of traits, or core elements. Knowing what these traits look like makes it easier to identify jazz dance. The main characteristics of jazz dance are that it is rhythm driven, in dialogue with gravity, directly expressive, and embraces individual style.

> ## DID YOU KNOW?
>
> Contrary to the popular myth that jazz dance came from ballet, jazz dance existed for many years before ballet-trained dancers began to adopt it. But the version of jazz dance taught in many academic dance settings today has strong ballet and modern influences.

Rhythm Driven

Jazz dance is propelled by dynamic and often syncopated rhythms. As a rhythm-driven dance form, dynamics, accents, and syncopation predominate.

Dynamics

Dynamics in jazz dance are often expressed through six phrase types: even, percussive, impact, impulse, swing, and vibratory. If you were to begin with your right arm crossed in front of your body over to your left side at about shoulder height and then moved it, again across the body, to your right side with a sustained, even motion, you would be using an **even** dynamic. This use of energy is uncommon in jazz dance. It looks boring. Now do the same motion but instead of using an even dynamic, try a strong, energetic, **percussive** movement. Percussive phrasing is precise and sharp and works well in synchronized movement. Often, cheerleaders and dance teams consistently stick to this one dynamic. Jazz dance uses a wide array of dynamics. It would be dull if dancers stuck to either one or even both of these phrase types.

Now start with your arm across your body as you did with even and percussive dynamics. This time, start easy and slow but speed up and get stronger along the way until you reach full speed and strength at the end of the movement. This attack of energy is called **impact** phrasing. You build from beginning to end, where you hit a wall with full force. Impact creates excitement because of the increase in energy in the movement. Another exciting phrase type for jazz dance, **impulse**, is the opposite of impact. It starts with a pulse of energy but then, instead of just stopping as it does at the end of impact and percussive, it gradually fades away.

Next are the two dynamics that cycle back and forth: swing and vibratory. Hold your right arm over to the left side of your body as you did before. This time, instead of following a straight line at shoulder height, let your arm drop down and swing in front of you. Gravity pulls the arm down in front, picking up speed as you cross at the bottom. Then, as the arm begins to rise up, gravity works to slow the arm down and suspend it. **Swing** phrasing oscillates between moments of full release and moments of suspension. In contrast, **vibratory** phrasing alternates in quick, rapidly changing patterns. Hold your hand to the side one more time and move it across the body to the right, this time, shaking the hand to make a quivering motion as you do so.

With your arsenal of phrase types ready (even, percussive, impact, impulse, swing, and vibratory), you are ready to be a dynamic jazz dancer. Jazz dancers do not stop there. Next, they layer accents on top of these phrase types.

ACTIVITY

SIX PHRASE TYPES

Choose a movement, any movement. It can be a gesture with your arm, a shrug of your shoulders, or a turn of your head. Now try this one movement with all six phrase types: even, percussive, impact, impulse, swing, and vibratory. See which type most interests you.

Accents

Imagine for a second watching a video of Michael Jackson performing. He stands in profile and on the beat looks sharply toward the audience. Usually he benefits from some wonderful sound effect that makes this exciting, but he also does something else rhythmically. He uses oppositional accents: a preparation in the opposite direction of the desired accent. So, in the preceding case, before he looks at the audience, he looks away from them slightly before whipping his head in their direction, creating a sharper, dynamically powerful movement. Dynamics and accents combined make jazz dance pop and sizzle, but jazz dancers can add one more aspect to join with those two to become more rhythm driven: **syncopation**.

Syncopation

Jazz music uses syncopation, the placing of accents unexpectedly on the upbeat rather than the downbeat. Most popular music today does not use syncopation as jazz music does. Nevertheless, jazz dancers continue to find ways to syncopate the rhythms of their bodies. Karen Hubbard, an associate professor of dance at the University of North Carolina in Charlotte who specializes in authentic jazz, describes jazz dance as being mostly initiated through the syncopated actions of the feet.

Imagine taking three steps forward, starting with your right foot, then your left, and then your right again while following the rhythm 1 and 2. This pattern is a duple meter; the beat is divided into two because the "and" falls exactly in the middle of 1 and 2. Divide the counts into triple meter. Instead of 1 and 2, you now have to count it 1 and a 2. This rhythm includes an extra beat. Fix that by removing the "and" and counting the rhythm 1 a 2. Now try the three steps forward with the new syncopated rhythm, stepping right, left, right. By altering even rhythms by sliding the one beat over closer to the downbeat, jazz dancers turn steady rhythms into exciting, dynamic ones using syncopation.

Jazz, as a rhythm-driven form, not only embraces dynamics, accents, and syncopation but also has a two-way relationship with gravity.

> ### ACTIVITY
>
> #### SYNCOPATED CLAPPING
>
> With a partner, clap these two rhythms. Partner A claps 1 and 2 3 4, 5 and 6 7 8. Partner B claps 1 2 3 and 4, 5 6 7 and 8. Put the two rhythms together. Then slide the one beat over closer to the downbeat to syncopate it. Partner A claps 1 a2 3 4, 5 a6 7 8, while partner B claps 1 2 3 a4, 5 6 7 a8.

Dialogue with Gravity

Jazz dance often employs a grounded, low center of gravity. Jazz dance engages a dialogue with gravity, embracing weight, processing it, and then sending it out into space energetically. For the jazz dancer, the dialog with gravity is a two-way conversation in which the dancer drops into a low center of gravity and then uses the rebound energy that comes up from the ground. This movement contrasts with simply bending the knees and straightening them, which does not work with gravity, but rather against it. Jazz dance specifically releases into gravity, pulls energy from the reaction, processes it, and then uses it for dynamic results.

In a jazz leap, the dancer drops into gravity for the preparation, takes to the air, and explodes at the top of the leap. When you see a dancer explode at the peak of leaps or kicks, you are probably watching jazz dance, especially if the dancer uses direct expressiveness.

Direct Expressiveness

Like jazz music that originally strived to affect the live audience by getting them to stand up and dance, jazz dance traditionally uses direct expressiveness of personal feeling between dancers and sometimes with the audience. Natural expressions of personal feeling show the emotions of the dancer, rather than holding her or him back. Besides being directly expressive with their feelings, jazz dancers are also directly expressive with their bodies, dancing with abandon, whether it is a dance of joy or power or seduction. Jazz dancers often use eye contact to communicate and relate with each other and even with the audience in some forms of jazz dance. Because jazz dancers directly express themselves, each dancer inevitably brings his or her own individual style to dancing.

Individual Style

In jazz dance class you will be encouraged to take a movement and make it your own. With roots in social dance, individual style naturally exists throughout jazz dance. Early jazz dancer Pepsi Bethel said that no two jazz dancers are the same; each brings individuality to the dance. As you make it your own, you will develop a personal sense of style and artistry. Just as jazz music included improvisation, jazz dance invites an element of improvisation in your stylistic interpretation. In this way, individual style and artistry go hand in hand in learning jazz dance.

Jazz dance exhibits an inherent democracy by valuing the individual within the group. Jazz dancers express themselves individually while working cooperatively in a large group, following along but expressing their unique voices. Finding balance between the given dance steps and the dancer's individual style creates an artistically nuanced approach to jazz dance. Great jazz dancers can often do the same combination or dance in the exact style of the choreographer and then move fluidly into their own personal style. An extension of individual style with similar roots in social dancing, the ability to free-style, or improvise, often finds its way into jazz dances in which the choreographer plans for the dancers to improvise select portions, making it blend seamlessly with the preplanned choreography.

Think of jazz dance as a large family. Whether we are talking about steps like the sugar from authentic early jazz, barrel turns from musical theater jazz, contractions from modern concert jazz, or the latest craze in hip-hop dance, the family resemblance holds these steps together, from across the decades. If you see dance performed with a strong rhythmic focus, in dialogue with gravity, using direct expression, and embracing individual style, chances are it falls somewhere in the jazz dance family tree. Now that you know what jazz dance looks like, you need to learn the benefits that make it worth studying.

These jazz dance students are performing the Stagger jazz arm isolation sequence with classical second position legs and third position arms with jazz hands. Isolations build coordination and logical-spatial skills.

BENEFITS OF STUDYING JAZZ DANCE

The quickest answer to the question, "Why study jazz dance?" is that it is joyful. Jazz dance grew out of the social dance forms that young people had used over many decades. It is what people do when they are celebrating, relaxing, and enjoying themselves. Jazz dance today, in all its forms, still maintains that joyous excitement. But studying jazz dance offers benefits beyond just sheer enjoyment, such as physical fitness, artistic expression, and practical cross-training skills for aspiring dancers.

Health and Physical Fitness

The health and physical fitness benefits of jazz dance include increased strength, flexibility, coordination, and endurance. The athletic, full-bodied nature of jazz dance develops arm strength from floor work, leg strength from jumps, and core strength from coordinating the limbs. Jazz dance classes consist of stretching sequences that lengthen the larger muscles of the legs and lower back. Increased flexibility and range of motion in the hips, shoulders, and spine commonly develop from jazz dance training. Challenging steps and combinations, in which the upper and lower body parallel and

SAFETY TIP

As a dance student, you need to be able to distinguish good pain from bad pain. Good pain comes from strength, stretching, and endurance exercises that expand the ability of the body. These pains may feel uncomfortable, but they are beneficial. Bad pain comes from pushing the body too far too fast, and it leads to injury. These pains tend to be sharp and sudden. Listen to your body to find the edge of good pain and do not go past it.

contrast each other in numerous ways, create increased coordination in jazz dancers. Remember the old challenge to rub your head and pat your tummy? That task becomes simple for jazz dancers who learn complex rhythmic patterns. Besides the strength, flexibility, and coordination developed in jazz dance, the infectious, high-energy rhythmic music of a jazz dance class leads to increased endurance and stamina.

Artistic Expression

Alongside the physical benefits of jazz dance, the ability to express the creative self through movement allows a full-bodied approach to sharing personal emotions and artistic insights. Because the body explores physical movement in jazz dance class while simultaneously allowing a free flow of personal expression, both a release and a strengthening of the mind–body connection occur. Euphoric feelings that jazz dancers sometimes refer to as a rush or high often result.

Cross-Training

Besides gaining the physical and emotional benefits of studying jazz dance, dancers who study other forms of dance gain in further practical ways. The emphasis in jazz dance on rhythmic complexity and dynamic performance helps ballet and modern dancers enhance their ability as dancers. Although ballet training develops incredible grace, the codified technique often becomes rhythmically predictable and dynamically smooth. Modern dance training often creates organically connected and grounded dancers who may become restricted dynamically. Ballet and modern dancers trained in jazz dance add intricate rhythmic coordination and the ability to add dynamic performance qualities to their range, making jazz dance an important part of training for versatile dancers. Combining these practical skills for aspiring dancers with enhanced physical fitness, artistic expression, and an overall joyful experience provides a self-evident answer to the question, "Why study jazz dance?" Now that you have learned the definition of jazz dance and reviewed the benefits, you will want to know the rules of class.

JAZZ DANCE CLASS EXPECTATIONS AND ETIQUETTE

The expectations and etiquette expected of any jazz dance student come from an understanding of one simple concept: respect. They exist so that you show respect for the studio space; respect for others; respect for the teacher, the musician, and the art form; and, most important, respect for yourself.

You show respect for the studio space by first leaving all food, drink, and gum outside the studio (sometimes exceptions are made for water bottles). You also show respect for the studio space by keeping your personal belongings in your bag and stowed neatly away. Keeping a safe studio environment free from loose items that can be tripped and slipped on is everyone's responsibility. By extension, keeping trash in its proper place obviously displays respect for the shared studio space. Aside from keeping things out of the studio space that should not be there, you also show respect by how you enter class. Dancers walk into class quietly and respectfully. Once in the studio, you continue to show respect by never leaning on or hanging on the barres. Barres are devices commonly used in ballet classes and occasionally in jazz dance class to provide balance. They may be attached to the walls or be free standing and portable. You can sum up the etiquette for showing respect for the studio space simply as this: Keep things where they belong and use things only for what they are intended.

Respect for others begins before you step into class. If you arrive late and class has already begun, show respect for others by waiting at the door for the teacher to invite you in, which usually happens during a pause between exercises. Then enter quickly and quietly to show respect for your classmates who are already engaged in the class. During class, show respect for your classmates by waiting quietly while the teacher gives instructions and when waiting for your turn to go across the floor. When going across the floor, be ready to go when it is your turn. You also show respect for others by being aware of their personal space. Make room for those taking their turn going across the floor or practicing a combination when you are waiting.

Displaying respect for the teacher, the musician, and the art form occurs in many ways. First, being properly dressed for class shows the teacher that you take the class and its rules seriously. Appropriate dress also ensures that the teacher can give you corrections because she or he can see when you make mistakes. You also show respect by making eye contact with the teacher and avoiding crossed arms or hands on the hips while listening to instructions and corrections. Studies in body language show that when you cross your arms you take in less information. When you place your hands on your hips, your body is resting rather than being engaged in the work.

Occasionally, you may have to leave the studio during a class. You show the teacher respect by asking quietly before leaving the room. Upon returning, you enter quietly and go to the back of the room, never walking through the dancers taking class. While taking class, you show respect by completing every exercise fully, without making a display of your aggravation and frustration, even when it may be present. Finally, although each teacher has a different ritual for the end of class, students commonly applaud the musician and the teacher at the end to show respect for their time and energy. Often, you personally thank the musician and teacher before leaving the studio.

You show respect for yourself by showing up to class on time and by being properly dressed. After all, you are going to get the most out of class if you are on time and ready to move. Ultimately, every aspect of respect comes down to self-respect. If you show respect for the studio space, for others, for the teacher, for the musician, and for the art form, you are going to get the most out of your jazz dance class.

SUMMARY

Now you know that jazz dance is rhythm driven, in dialogue with gravity, directly expressive, and embracing of individual style. You learned that reasons for studying jazz dance include health and physical fitness, artistic expression, and cross-training. You also learned that the expectations and etiquette of jazz dance class require respect for the studio space, teacher, musician, art form, and yourself. With this understanding, you are one step closer to becoming that smiling dancer grooving to infectiously rhythmic music. In chapter 2 we will look at what exactly to wear; how to prepare physically and mentally for jazz dance class; what to expect from the class structure; and what the specific roles are for the teacher, student, and musician. In no time, you will be kicking your leg on the accent of the beat, spinning around, and jumping joyously into the air.

To find supplementary materials for this chapter, such as learning activities, e-journal assignments, and web links, visit the web resource at www.HumanKinetics.com/BeginningJazzDance.

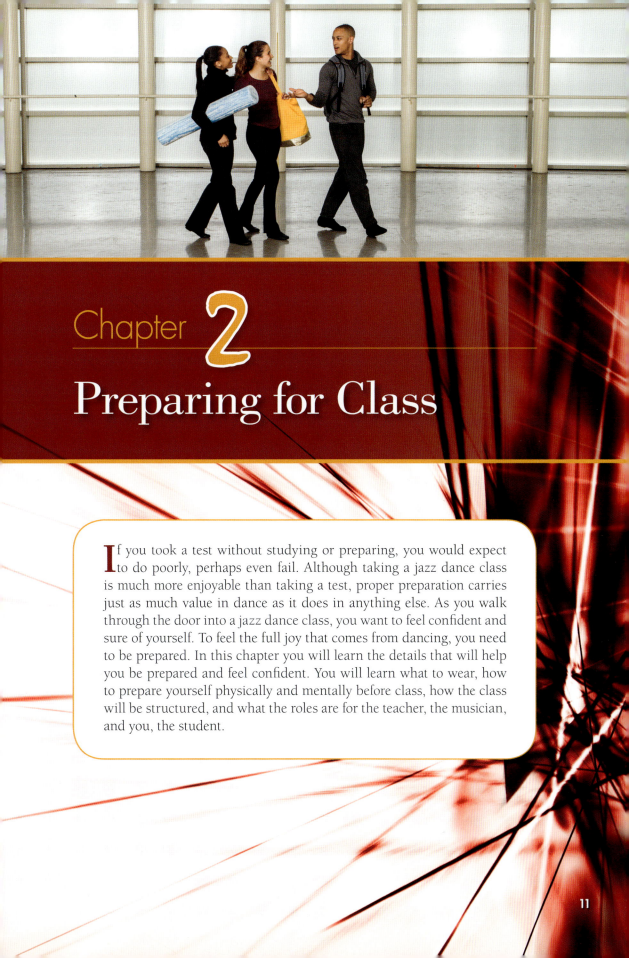

Chapter 2

Preparing for Class

If you took a test without studying or preparing, you would expect to do poorly, perhaps even fail. Although taking a jazz dance class is much more enjoyable than taking a test, proper preparation carries just as much value in dance as it does in anything else. As you walk through the door into a jazz dance class, you want to feel confident and sure of yourself. To feel the full joy that comes from dancing, you need to be prepared. In this chapter you will learn the details that will help you be prepared and feel confident. You will learn what to wear, how to prepare yourself physically and mentally before class, how the class will be structured, and what the roles are for the teacher, the musician, and you, the student.

DRESSING FOR CLASS

Proper attire in dance class serves three main purposes: It displays respect by showing your teacher and classmates that you are serious about learning, it promotes safety by ensuring that your attire does not add to the risk of injury, and it aids learning by allowing the teacher to see your exact body lines and movements so that you can receive effective feedback.

Attire for Women

For women, leotards (or other appropriate dance tops) and tights or dance shorts are appropriate, along with a sports bra if necessary. No distracting or potentially dangerous jewelry should be worn. Anything that dangles can be caught while moving. Remove all necklaces, bracelets, anklets, and earrings that dangle below the earlobe. Hair must be pulled away from the face and secured. Often, you may wear warm-up clothing at the beginning of class as long as it is sufficiently form fitting for the teacher to see your body and alignment. Warm-up clothing usually consists of fitted shirts and jazz pants or athletic pants. You should be willing and able to remove the outer layers when requested.

Attire for Men

Men should wear black jazz pants, tights, or dance shorts and a solid, fitted T-shirt. A dance belt is required for all men. The rules for women concerning jewelry, hair, and warm-up clothing apply equally to men.

Dance students should warm up in proper attire: jazz pants, jazz shoes, leotards or form-fitting tops, with hair secured away from their faces and no jewelry. This helps the learning process because students and teachers can clearly see the body at work.

Jazz Shoes

Check with the teacher to learn whether she or he prefers you to start class with shoes or in bare feet. Students commonly begin in bare feet and put on jazz shoes after the warm-up. Some classes require the women to wear character shoes. Each teacher has specific preferences for jazz shoes, so you should check with the instructor before class begins to learn which type of shoe is required.

For most jazz dance classes, a soft-soled flexible black jazz shoe is recommended. Teachers who work in musical theater jazz dance styles in which the women are predominantly costumed in skirts with tan tights may require the women to wear tan jazz shoes, or even heeled character shoes. In contrast, teachers who work in street- or hip-hop-influenced styles of jazz dance may require black jazz sneakers that look like athletic shoes but have a more flexible sole.

CARRYING DANCE GEAR

Dancers carry a dance bag with them to hold their shoes and other items they need in class. Your dance bag should include a small towel in case you leave any sweat spots on the floor. With the amount of work done on the floor in a jazz dance class, sometimes you cannot avoid creating a slick spot from sweat. Etiquette requires you to have a small towel handy to wipe up any wet spots so that others do not slip on them.

Working hard in jazz dance class leads you to sweat, making deodorant another necessity in your dance bag. For general foot care, you should carry adhesive bandages and athletic tape in case any small injuries occur. You should keep your toenails clipped, so carrying nail clippers in your dance bag is necessary. Additionally, pain

From left to right: black lace-up oxford, tan slip-on oxford, black split sole Padini-style, tan character shoe, black jazz sneaker. The color of the shoe usually depends on the style of jazz. Black shoes are worn with pants or black tights and tan shoes with tan tights, which usually are worn with skirts.

relievers as well as small plastic bags to hold ice are essential. Your dance bag for jazz dance class would be incomplete without safety pins, hair ties, thin kneepads, a water bottle, and a light nutritious snack for after class.

With your dance bag packed, the right attire, jewelry removed, and your hair secured away from your face, you look the part of a jazz dance student and are ready to step into the studio with confidence. But wait—you need to do some other important things before class starts to ensure that you get the most out of the class.

PREPARING YOURSELF MENTALLY AND PHYSICALLY

While rushing from one class to the next, dance students easily forget that a personal warm-up is a vital ingredient to having a good class. Personal warm-ups are individual, but they usually consist of some centering, aerobic activity, and light stretching. Personal warm-ups are most effective when they include and progress from mental preparation to mind–body preparation to physical preparation.

> ### SAFETY TIP
> Light stretching helps you prepare your joints and muscles for physical activity and increases your awareness of how your body feels in the moment. Light stretching consists of exploring the range of motion of the body without exerting muscular effort or dynamic force. Deep stretching puts more demands on the muscles, so you should not attempt it until your body is thoroughly warmed up.

Mental Preparation

Transitioning from sitting for an hour in the academic class you just walked out of right into a dance class can be jarring to the mind and body. Taking time to center yourself mentally and then visualizing the work ahead can help you make the most out of your time, focus your mind, and release tension. In *Dance Imagery for Technique and Performance*, Eric Franklin (2014) notes that mental training is as important as physical training. In *Bounce*, Mathew Syed (2010) worked with leading sport psychologists over a decade to fine-tune a four-step approach to mental preparation:

1. Centering through deep breathing
2. Recalling past positive experiences
3. Visualizing what is upcoming
4. Finishing with positive affirmations

Centering

Before the dance class, take a moment to center yourself, perhaps by simply taking some deep breaths to clear your mind. **Centering** is the process of focusing the mind. If you have a meditation practice, this is a good time to do it. A simple breathing exercise for centering consists of sitting in a comfortable position and counting your breaths. Count the inhale as 1 and the exhale as 2. Do this until you get to 10 and then start over. As you count, focus only on the breath. As other thoughts, concerns, worries, or hopes come to mind, just notice them and let them pass as you come back to focus on counting your breaths. If you lose count, start over at 1. Centering helps you slow down and focus on how you are feeling at that moment. Jumping right into physical activity without centering can lead you to ignore signs that your body gives you, like sore muscles or excess tension. Ignoring these signals can lead to injury. One to five minutes of a centering exercise will help you focus your mind on the work you are about to do.

Recalling

After you are centered through a deep-breathing sequence, recall a positive experience you had in dance or movement. **Recalling** is a sport psychology technique that mentally prepares you for positive performance experiences by remembering past successes. Whether it is a prior class or the sensation you have dancing alone in your room, recalling alerts your neuromuscular system and primes your mind and body for positive experiences. Start by imagining that you are observing yourself in that past moment from a third-person point of view. Then transition yourself fully into the moment from a first-person point of view. To strengthen the imagery, try to recall all your senses from that moment: the sights, the sounds, the smells, the physical sensations, and the emotions you felt.

Visualizing

After you have centered through breathing and recalled positive imagery, visualization techniques can help prepare you for success in the class. **Visualization** is a mental preparation technique that uses the imagination to prepare the neuromuscular connection for upcoming tasks. Visualization techniques help further prime the pump by waking up the neuromuscular connections that you will call on in class to execute those same skills.

> ### ACTIVITY
>
> **VISUALIZATION**
>
> Try closing your eyes for a few minutes and visualize yourself in the class, doing everything well. Imagine every detail done perfectly. If you want to improve on an exercise or combination, visualize yourself doing it with great success.

Affirming

Finish the mental preparation sequence with positive affirmations. **Affirmations** are a sport psychology technique that creates necessary confidence. Sport psychology teaches that a healthy dose of optimism actually creates better results (Syed, 2010). Take the time not just to encourage yourself that you are going to do well but also to convince yourself of it. Suspend disbelief and dismiss your personal skeptic for the time being.

The combination of centering, recalling, visualizing, and affirming is an important part of the preparation for dance class that will lead you to growth and greater enjoyment. In addition to mental preparation, mind–body preparedness brings into focus several aspects of coordination that dancers specifically use.

Mind–Body Preparation

As a dancer, you will develop a heightened understanding of the mind–body relationship—how you sense the space around you, your body, and the relationships between your movement patterns. Including spatial sense, kinesthetic sense, and movement patterns in your personal warm-up connects your mind and body so that you can move with greater connection and coordination.

Spatial Sense

Spatial sense is awareness of space and the way in which objects, including the self and others, occupy space. Try this experiment: Close your eyes, extend your arms to the side, and make a fist with your pinky fingers extended. Now, bring the tips of your pinky fingers together. This task is surprisingly difficult. We do not often realize that our spatial sense can be off or varied, but we can improve it with practice.

By awakening your spatial sense in your personal warm-up, you prepare yourself to move with a connection and awareness for the space around you.

ACTIVITY

SPATIAL SENSE

To enliven your spatial sense, take 30 seconds to look around and notice the environment around you—the distance of the objects and the details of their size, shape, and color. Additionally, hold your hands out in front of you and notice the slight differences in the positions of the fingers, the shape of the hands, and the space between your body and hands.

Kinesthetic Sense

Kinesthetic sense is the awareness of the body and movement ability. Whereas spatial sense is the awareness of the body in space, kinesthetic sense is the understanding of the body in movement. Simply standing still for a moment and noticing where you are holding tension, what parts of the body feel calm, and what parts feel tense directs your attention to your kinesthetic sense. Exploring this awareness while moving provides important feedback about your body that you may tend to ignore in your day-to-day life. A good exercise to explore your kinesthetic sense is to lie on your back with your feet flexed so that your toes point toward the ceiling. Point and flex your feet and notice how that movement travels through the rest of your body, noting which body parts are still and which move.

By becoming aware of your kinesthetic sense, you notice the subtle movements and energies flowing through your body while moving.

Movement Patterns

The ability to observe movement patterns within the body helps you to accurately articulate as a dancer. Seeing the six patterns of connectivity within the body provides a framework for understanding movement (Hackney, 2002).

Breath connectivity is the relationship between breathing and movement. A natural flow of breath underlies all your movement. You never simply raise your arms. You are either raising your arms supported by an inhale and expansion of the torso or raising your arms supported by an exhale and collapsing of the torso. An awareness of breath connectivity allows you to let this naturally occurring support inform and influence your movement rather than being disconnected from it.

Core-distal connectivity is the relationship between the muscles of your torso as they support and provide stability for your limbs in space. Reaching out into space with an arm or leg without adequate core support leads to instability. To awaken your core-distal connectivity, raise your arms out into space away from your center while feeling the grounding support of your abdominal and upper back muscles, making sure that the shoulders do not lift toward the ears.

Head-tail connectivity is the relationship between the crown of your head and the tip of your tailbone. We tend to treat the cervical spine and head as separate from the rest of the spine. If your head and neck move without connection to your mid and lower spine (thoracic and lumbar), the coordination of your entire body is compromised. To awaken your head-tail connectivity, start from a standing position and roll down through the spine slowly, starting at the top of the head and working through each successive vertebra, paying special attention to avoid assisting the roll down by moving a group of vertebrae all at once.

Upper-lower connectivity is the relationship between the lower body (hips and legs) and the upper body (torso and arms). A strong, stable lower body—hips, legs, ankles, and feet—provides stability that allows an expressive and mobile upper body. Movement in which either both arms or both legs work symmetrically and simultaneously enlivens your upper-lower connectivity. Lying on your belly, reach out with your arms to the floor in front of you and then pull yourself to your hands. Reverse this action by pushing against the floor and sliding your body back away from your hands. For your lower body, simply jump on both feet, bending your knees before and after the jump. Feel your weight going into the floor as you push against it.

Body-half connectivity is the relationship between one side of your body and the other. This pattern occurs when one side of the body stabilizes to allow the other side to mobilize. Stand with your feet together and your arms at your side. Stabilize the left side of the body and then lift your right knee up and raise your right hand above your head. Move slowly and sense the relationship between the two sides.

Cross lateral connectivity is the relationship between diagonally opposing parts of your body. You can see cross lateral (also called oppositional) connectivity when you walk as you step forward with your right foot (lower right body) and swing your left arm forward (upper left body). Cross lateral connection combines upper-lower connectivity with body-half connectivity for a three-dimensional experience of space. Lie on your back in a giant letter X with your legs and arms extended. Bring your right elbow and left knee together, with both limbs bent, in front of your body. Return to the X. Repeat on the other side.

An awareness of spatial sense, kinesthetic sense, and movement patterns combined with mental preparation readies your body for dance class in ways that will lead to accelerated growth, in contrast to going without the preparation. Physical preparation, which includes the direct use of the muscular and cardiovascular systems, completes the personal warm-up.

Physical Preparation

After you are mentally prepared and have awakened the mind–body connection, you need to get your heart rate up. Avoid the urge to just sit and stretch. Cold muscles do not stretch well. Get your blood flowing by performing some light aerobic activity, such as jogging, jumping jacks, or even vigorous walking on the way to class. With your blood flowing and your muscles warm, do some light stretching and strengthening exercises, paying close attention to places that need the most work. Make sure that your personal warm-up contains a balance of strength, endurance, and flexibility exercises.

Strength

Strength is the ability for the muscle to produce a maximal force on one occasion. Dancers use a mix of power and control. **Power** is the explosive (speed-related) aspect of muscular strength. Jumps in jazz dance class require the use of power generated from the legs. Athletic-bodied students with limited flexibility tend to focus their personal warm-ups on strength activities and do little stretching, which they need the most. Flexible-bodied students tend to sit and stretch when more strength and conditioning would be most beneficial for them. Most people want to do a personal warm-up by doing what feels good to them instead of doing what they need. If strength is your weakness, consider devoting the second half of your personal warm-up to strengthening activities.

Endurance

Endurance is the ability to produce continuous movement through muscular and cardiovascular conditioning. Extending the legs in the air or lowering the body slowly to the floor with weight on the arms is an example of controlled muscular endurance in the jazz dance class. Jazz dance students require both muscular endurance and cardiovascular endurance in the form of aerobic fitness and anaerobic fitness. **Aerobic fitness** is associated with moderate, long-term levels of activity. **Anaerobic fitness** is associated with high-intensity, maximal, short bursts of activity. If endurance and stamina are your personal weaknesses, aerobic activities, such as jogging, cycling, swimming, or aerobics exercise classes will greatly increase your success in the dance studio.

Flexibility

Flexibility is the range of motion at a joint in association with the pliability of a muscle. The range of motion available to a dancer not only creates many of the exciting visual images dancers are known for but also helps prevent injury. Care should be taken not to force your body into a stretch or bounce because doing so may strain the muscles. If flexibility is your weakness, remember to get the blood flowing through light aerobic activity before spending the second half of your personal warm-up on stretching. For example, if you have tight hamstrings after centering, aerobic activity, and light stretching, spend the final few minutes just stretching your hamstrings.

> ### SAFETY TIP
> Hypermobility, or too much mobility in a joint, can also cause injuries in dancers. If your flexibility and mobility are extreme or are not balanced by proper strength, injuries may occur. Good physical preparation takes into account a balance between flexibility and strength.

To be in a position to have the most positive experience in class, you should begin by preparing mentally through centering, recalling, visualizing, and affirming. Then, prepare your mind–body connection through exploring spatial sense, kinesthetic sense, and movement patterns. Finish the warm-up with physical preparation through strength, endurance, and flexibility exercises. Above all, make sure that your personal warm-up is just that—personal. Address any issues you have. With your mind and body prepared and wearing the right attire, you are ready to get the most you can out of your jazz dance class.

JAZZ DANCE CLASS STRUCTURE

Just as jazz dance respects the idea of individual style, each jazz dance teacher brings his or her unique experience and personality to the class. You will find, however, that certain structures are consistent from one class to the next. The jazz dance class starts with a warm-up that includes exercises that engage the entire body from head to toe while warming the major muscle groups of the legs, torso, and arms. Isolations and coordination exercises often follow, and the warm-up culminates in conditioning exercises that stretch and strengthen the body. From there, the class builds various skills in center work and by doing progressions across the floor. The last portion of class is dedicated to learning a combination. At the end, you will cool down with some kind of closing sequence that serves not only to take the heart rate back to a normal state but also to show respect for your teacher, classmates, and musicians for dance.

Warm-Up

In jazz dance class, the **warm-up** is a series of exercises performed at the beginning of the class to awaken the body by getting blood flowing to all the major muscle groups of the torso, legs, and arms. In addition, the warm-up consists of core exercises that develop, stretch, and strengthen the group of muscles supporting the trunk, back, abdominals, shoulders, hips, and ribs. A strong core stabilizes and connects the torso to the lower body. This stabilization creates an expressive, mobile torso that is unique to jazz dance in which movements are often generated from this supple yet dynamic core. Core strength also helps with height in aerial movements, support in floor work and inversions, and control in turns. Throughout the term, the warm-up exercises may expand to include additional exercises and their variations to support your learning in other parts of the jazz dance class.

Isolations

Typically, the next section of a jazz dance class is isolations. **Isolations** are a series of exercises that mobilize one body part at a time to develop refined, specific control. The ribs, shoulders, hips, arms, legs, head, feet, and hands are worked individually to increase coordination and mobility. At the end of isolations, separate isolations combine together to reconnect the various parts of the body, creating a layered combination that develops coordination.

At the end of the isolations, coordination exercises are usually done. **Coordination exercises** are performed to integrate the isolated body parts while developing correct posture, coordination of leg and arm movements, and articulation of the feet and ankles. These exercises may include jazz dance versions of ballet plié and tendu exercises to ground the body and warm up the feet. Alternately, these exercises may appear later in the class structure during exercises in the center.

> ### DID YOU KNOW?
>
> Isolations as they are performed in most jazz dance classes today come from the technique of Jack Cole, who studied Indian classical dance and integrated the isolated head, arm, and rib movements into his jazz dance class.

Conditioning

The next section of jazz dance class consists of conditioning exercises. **Conditioning exercises** are a sequence of movements that develop muscular strength (the ability for the muscle to produce maximal force on one occasion), muscular endurance (the ability of a muscle to produce continuous movement), and flexibility (the range of motion at a joint in association with the pliability of a muscle). Specifically, conditioning exercises increase flexibility of the legs and spine while strengthening the core, leg, and arm muscles. For the jazz dancer, increased flexibility leads to greater range of motion, and increased strength leads to greater stability that protects the integrity of the joints. Usually, this exercise completes the first half of the jazz dance

These jazz dance students are in a jazz fourth position of the feet performing a rib isolation exercise. The wide stance and low-to-the-ground character of jazz dance distinguishes it from other dance forms and makes it a soulful and powerful form of expression.

class. From here, the teacher will instruct you to prepare for center work or move to the side of the room to begin progressions across the floor.

Exercises in the Center

Exercises in the center are a series of exercises performed in the center of the studio that build specific skill sets and movement vocabulary specific to jazz dance. These exercises focus on quick changes of weight; sharp changes of direction; level changes; bending, extending, and rotating joint actions; spiraling of the spine; gestures of the limbs; or any combination of those. Exercises in the center repeat jazz steps in a variety of combinations.

Exercises Across the Floor

Exercises across the floor are a series of exercises that dancers perform while moving across the floor. The exercises incorporate learned movement vocabulary and focus on traveling through space, from one point to another. In jazz dance, progressions include stylized walks, weight changes, direction changes, kicks, turns, elevations, and floor work. Often, each progression develops on the one before it, building movement phrases that can be incorporated in a combination later in class.

Combinations

The exercises throughout the jazz dance class culminate in a combination. A **combination** is an extended movement sequence that combines the skills being worked on in class and explores specific stylistic and performance aspects of jazz dance. Combinations can be in a variety of jazz dance styles and may consist of learning choreography from an established dance.

Cool-Down

After the combination, the jazz dance class ends with a cool-down. A **cool-down** is a sequence at the end of class designed to slow the heart rate and gently stretch the muscles that have been worked, relieving excess tension. Besides cooling down the muscles and reducing the heart rate, the cool-down may be used to reconnect the mind and body; provide a sense of group cohesiveness; and give respect for fellow classmates, musicians, and teachers. Depending on the tradition that your particular teacher follows, after the cool-down students may applaud and then individually say thank you to the teacher and musician for dance.

ROLES OF THE TEACHER, MUSICIAN, AND STUDENTS

A successful dance class depends on collaboration between the teacher, the musician for dance, and the students. All have specific responsibilities that, when embraced, add to the whole. The teacher's role in the classroom is to create the best atmosphere possible in which to learn. To do this, the teacher has a number of responsibilities. The teacher starts class by taking attendance and stating any expectations for the class. At this time, the teacher checks that all students are adhering to the proper dress code for safety in the class. The teacher will have a class prepared for the students and is responsible for starting on time, moving the class along in an orderly fashion, and finishing on time.

If you are fortunate enough to have a live musician for dance in class, the musician will be responsible for accompanying the class with various styles of music and tempos to fit the individual exercises and combinations. The musician for dance also helps with questions and lessons regarding musicality and rhythms. She or he works with the teacher to keep the class moving and keep the energy of the class flowing.

As a student, if you come into the studio properly dressed, mentally focused, and physically warmed up, you have already met many of your responsibilities. During the class, remembering to respect the studio space, your classmates, the teacher, and the musician ensures that you are doing your part so that you and others get the most out of the class. In addition, you need to be eager and open, listening and watching throughout the class to glean every little correction and tip you can. Imagine that every correction is specifically for you, even when the teacher directs it toward another student or to the class in general. Then, when class ends, make sure you leave the room as clean as it was when you came in, returning everything to its proper place. If portable barres or any props were used, return them to their assigned places away from the center of the studio.

SUMMARY

When you walk into the jazz dance class, you can now feel prepared. You know what the appropriate attire is for females and males, what type of shoes to wear, and what to carry in your dance bag. You also know the four steps of mental preparation: center, recall, visualize, and affirm. You understand that your personal warm-up should include physical exercises that address strength, endurance, and flexibility and that mind–body exercises help you develop spatial sense, kinesthetic sense, and movement patterns. By knowing the structure of the jazz dance class and the reason for each exercise, you are better prepared to get the most from your class. Finally, an understanding of the roles of the teacher, musician, and student ensures that you can walk into class confidently, ready to explore jazz dance openly and eagerly. But before you jump into class, we need to go over some health and safety considerations, which are the focus of chapter 3.

To find supplementary materials for this chapter, such as learning activities, e-journal assignments, and web links, visit the web resource at **www.HumanKinetics.com/BeginningJazzDance.**

WEB RESOURCE

Chapter 3

Safety and Health

You now know what to expect when you walk into the jazz dance class and what the teacher expects of you. The next question to answer is, "Do you know what to expect from your body?" Jazz dance is an exciting and physically demanding activity. An understanding of proper health, nutrition, and injury prevention techniques is key to preparing you to have an enjoyable experience in jazz dance class. After all, you cannot enjoy moving if you fear for your safety or have to sit out of class because of an injury. With proper preparation and a thorough understanding of safety and health issues, your time in the studio can be focused on the joy of experiencing the rhythms and the movement. In this chapter you will learn the safety and health information that will support you in getting the most from your dance classes. You will learn how to be safe in the studio environment; what you can do personally to keep yourself safe; how to avoid injuries; and how proper nutrition, hydration, and rest can enhance your learning.

STUDIO SAFETY

Because dancers are leaping and twirling around the dance studio, the studio needs to be kept safe to prevent accidents. An innocently misplaced piece of equipment or bag can be a hazard that causes a dancer to trip and twist an ankle. A slick spot on the floor can cause a dancer to slip and fall. The responsibility for awareness of general studio safety practices falls on everyone in the dance classroom.

Equipment

Both dance equipment and personal equipment must be clear from the dance floor. In the studio, portable barres from ballet class may cause a hazard if they are not put neatly away to the side. If portable barres are in the studio space, make sure that they are off to the side, taking up as little space as possible. If chairs are in the room, either remove them or put them in a place against a wall where they will be clear from dancers taking class. Dancers sometimes bring personal equipment, such as dance bags and shoes, into the studio. In an ideal situation, these would all be left outside the studio in a locker. If this is not possible, make sure that your personal equipment is neatly stored in a place out of the way of where dancers will be moving.

Floors

Keeping the floor clear of equipment is only half of the equation for having a safe dance floor. The floor surface in a dance studio is designed to provide an appropriate amount of friction for safe dancing. Slick spots develop from sweat, body lotions,

Dancers should do their personal warm-ups in a cleared space before the start of the class.

powder, water, and the use of rosin. Responsible, respectful dancers carry towels to wipe up any sweat they may leave on the floor.

Avoid using body lotions and powders that leave residue on the floor. Just like sweat, drops of water from water bottles that are absentmindedly left on the floor create a hazard. Only a small amount can cause a sure-footed dancer to slip on a wet spot. Be mindful of your water bottle in the studio and understand that condensation tends to form and then drip down the outside of the bottle, leaving a puddle.

Rosin is a popular resin used by some dancers, especially ballet dancers, when they think that the dance floor is slippery. It was originally intended for wooden dance floors that tend to be slick. Most stages and dance studios today use a vinyl floor covering that creates more friction than wooden floors and therefore eliminates the need for rosin. In fact, the use of rosin on vinyl flooring creates slick spots. Avoiding the use of rosin is the safest practice for everyone using the floor and helps ensure a long life for the surface.

With portable barres, chairs, dance bags, water bottles, and shoes safely stored and the dance floor free of slick spots, you take dance class with confidence that your surroundings are safe. But some personal safety precautions remain to consider.

PERSONAL SAFETY

As a jazz dance student, you need to take some important personal safety steps before taking your first steps in the studio. Besides the personal warm-up discussed in chapter 2, an understanding of personal space and communication of personal health information to the teacher are important to your safety.

Personal Space

In the jazz dance class, you move quickly and energetically in close proximity to other dancers. Awareness of your personal space helps prevent accidents. **Personal space** is the area surrounding you, including the distance between yourself and others. **General space** is the area of the studio or stage. When a dancer loses awareness of his or her personal space and crosses into the personal space of a fellow dancer, especially while moving quickly and energetically, the risk of injury from tripping or colliding greatly increases. As a jazz dance student, you have to maintain a spatial sense of where others are in the room in relation to you. Maintaining proper distance between yourself and others in general space allows you and the other dancers to move freely without fear of personal injury.

Personal Health Information

If you have any personal health issues that might affect your performance in class during rigorous physical activity, you need to share that with the teacher. You can either contact the teacher before the beginning of the course or talk to her or him briefly before class begins. The teacher will then be prepared to handle any situations that might unexpectedly occur. In addition, the teacher may suggest adjustments or alternatives to exercises that might be problematic because of the issue.

Your personal warm-up, awareness of personal space, and communication of relevant personal health information all add to your personal safety in the jazz dance class. They are pivotal steps to preventing injuries. But they do not suffice in injury prevention. An understanding of how your body works is necessary.

BASIC ANATOMY AND KINESIOLOGY

In jazz dance, enjoying the activity depends on your understanding of your body and the way that it moves. The study of anatomy, the bones and muscles, couples with the study of kinesiology, the movement of the body.

Basic Anatomy

To move your body safely, you need to know something about it. For jazz dance, a clear understanding of your skeletal and muscular systems helps you move intelligently.

Skeletal System

Just as a house needs a frame to hold up the walls, your body needs a skeleton to hold it together (see figure 3.1). Your skeleton consists of 206 bones that provide the foundation for your movement capacity, dictating both your potential and your limitations. **Joints** are the places where two or more bones interact. The three main types of joints important to jazz dancers are ball-and-socket, hinge, and gliding joints.

Muscular System

Your muscular system works in tandem with your skeletal system to create movement (see figure 3.2). The muscles act on the bones at the joints. **Dynamic contractions** occur when the length of the muscle changes. The two types of dynamic contractions are **concentric contraction**, a shortening of the muscle to create movement, and **eccentric contraction**, a lengthening of the muscle to create movement.

The muscles work together to create complex movement in jazz dance. **Agonist muscles** contract to produce movement. For example, when you bend at the elbow, your biceps muscle concentrically contracts. **Antagonist muscles** oppose the primary movers. When your biceps muscle (agonist) contracts, your triceps muscle (antagonist) relaxes and lengthens.

The skeletal and muscular systems combine to provide a wealth of movement potential. In jazz dance, understanding the basics of your skeletal and muscular systems provides a foundation for discovering coordinated and smooth body movement.

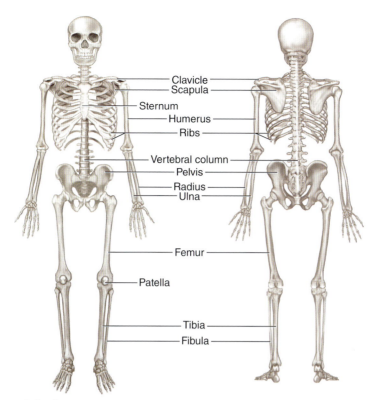

Figure 3.1 Skeletal system.

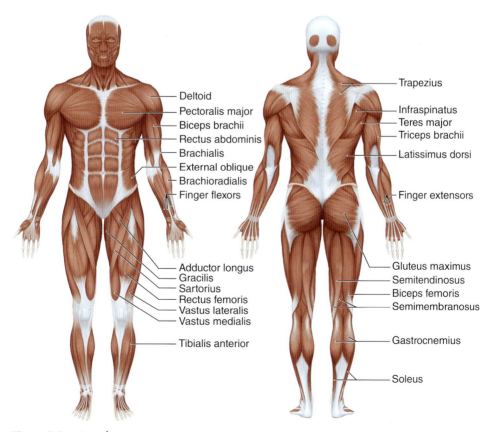

Figure 3.2 Muscular system.

Basic Kinesiology

Knowing your skeleton and muscles is an important, but incomplete, step in understanding how the body moves. **Kinesiology** is the science of human motion. Information about how the most common joints function and how the body moves in relation to space will complement your understanding of anatomy.

Joint Movements

The three main types of joints to know for jazz dance each have a different function. A **ball-and-socket joint** consists of a bone with a rounded end meeting up with a cup-shaped bone, allowing a circular range of motion. Your shoulder and hip joints are examples of this type. Both your shoulders and hips have the potential for circular movement because of this structure.

A **hinge joint** consists of a bone with a slight concave end meeting up with a bone with a slight convex end, allowing primarily extension and flexion. Your knees and elbows are examples of hinge joints. When you bend your knees or elbows, you are flexing the joint. When you straighten your knees or elbows, you are extending them.

A **gliding joint** consists of two bones meeting up with mostly flat surfaces. Gliding joints allow only a small amount of movement. The spine is a gliding joint. Expecting your spine to behave as a hinge joint can lead to injury.

A balance of mobility and stability in your joints allows you to move freely and safely. By understanding both the potential and limitations in each joint type, you will value the importance of having joints that are both flexible and strong.

Planes

Your body has the potential to move in three planes of action (see figure 3.3). You can move in only one plane at a time or in all three at once. A **plane** is an imaginary flat surface that passes through the body. The lateral plane contains side-to-side movement. A door is in a lateral plane. An example of a turning movement in the lateral plane is a cartwheel. The sagittal plane contains front-to-back movement. A wheel is in a sagittal plane. Examples of turning movements in the sagittal plane are forward and backward rolls. The transverse plane contains movement that

ACTIVITY

EXPLORING PLANES

Explore swinging your arm in all three planes. Start in the sagittal plane by raising one arm overhead and dropping it in front of you and continuing all the way around, like a Ferris wheel. Let it swing in this circle a few times. Now return the arm overhead and let it drop away from your body in the lateral plane, swinging a few times. Then, hold the arm out to your side and twist your torso, swinging your arm in front of you then swinging it away from you as if you are clearing all the dishes from the top of a table in the transverse plane.

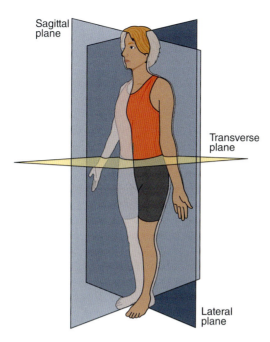

Sagittal
plane

Transverse
plane

Lateral
plane

Figure 3.3 Planes of movement.

revolves around your spine. The top of a table is in a transverse plane. An example of a turning movement in the transverse plane is spinning around in circles while staying in one spot on the floor.

Having a kinesiological understanding of how your muscles and bones work in relation to the various joint movements and the planes of action complements your knowledge of anatomy and prepares you to move safely. Although knowledge of the body and the way in which it moves will aid you in moving safely, it will not guarantee that you can avoid injuries. Next, we will explore what injuries to look out for and how to treat them.

PREVENTING AND TREATING COMMON JAZZ DANCE INJURIES

Avoiding injury is key to having a positive experience in jazz dance. Understanding your body and the way it moves are the beginning steps to injury prevention. The next important pieces of information are awareness of common jazz dance injuries and a method for dealing with injuries when they occur.

Jazz dance injuries to the ankle, lower leg, knee, and lower back differ in their causes and treatments. Correctly identifying and treating these injuries increases the speed of recovery.

These jazz dance students are helping a classmate with a minor ankle sprain by applying three steps of the PRICED method: protection, rest, and ice.

Ankle Pain

An **ankle sprain** is an injury to the ligaments surrounding the ankle. Ankle sprains are the most common injury for dancers (Clippinger, 2016). Ankle sprains often happen when a dancer comes out of a turn, comes down from a jump, or takes a misstep while performing intricate footwork. When coming out of a turn, the turning foot lowering from the position high on the metatarsals down to the floor is susceptible to rolling in or rolling out. This rolling in or rolling out can lead to injury to the ligaments surrounding the ankle. Similarly, when coming out of a jump, any small miscalculation in alignment of the ankle can result in an ankle sprain. Additionally, the quick, syncopated footwork in jazz dance can create situations in which missteps that end in ankle sprains are possible. When a dancer suffers an ankle sprain, he or she may hear a pop or feel a tearing sensation accompanied by immediate pain. Proper ankle alignment and strength while in movement helps prevent ankle sprains in jazz dancers.

Lower Leg Pain

Achilles tendinitis is another common injury for jazz dancers. Tendinitis is the inflammation of a tendon or its covering. The Achilles tendon, located behind the ankle, plays a roll in dance movements that involve jumping, rising up onto the metatarsals, or stretching the feet. The force on the Achilles tendon, especially when landing from jumps, can inflame it, causing discomfort and swelling. Proper rolling through the foot when coming out of and going into jumps and proper flooring greatly decrease the likelihood that a dancer will experience Achilles tendinitis.

Shin splints are a condition in which the dancer feels tenderness and discomfort on the front of the shin, especially when jumping. This condition is common among runners as well. Shin splints often result from a recent increase in activity. When starting a dance class for the first time or starting new exercises, shin splints may develop. To avoid shin splints, the dancer needs to strengthen the muscles in the front of the shin. Strengthening exercises should occur before shin splints happen or after they have gone away. Strengthening the muscles while still experiencing pain can further irritate the condition.

Knee Pain

Jumper's knee is an injury to tendons around the knee characterized by an aching feeling. Explosive use of the quadriceps muscle combined with poor use of the bending of the knee when taking off and landing contribute to the chances of developing this injury. In milder forms of the injury, you feel the ache until you are warmed up. When you are fully warmed up, the ache goes away, but it readily returns after activity has ended and the body begins to cool down. Having adequate strength in your quadriceps muscles, sufficient elasticity in the calf muscles, and proper flooring help prevent the development of jumper's knee.

Lower Back Pain

Lumbosacral strain is an injury to the small extensor muscles or ligaments of the spine. Extreme movements of the spine as well as repetitive stress over time cause them. A dancer with a lumbosacral strain may feel the back go into spasm on one or both sides of the spine. Because muscle stress and overexertion cause lumbosacral strains, dancers can minimize the chances of occurrences by paying close attention to their alignment and technique when lifting partners or executing extreme movements of the spine.

Mechanical low back pain is a condition involving localized lower back pain. Dancers with a swayback in posture or in the release of their lower backs in jumps and athletic movements may develop this generalized lower back pain. Muscular imbalances from the muscles supporting the lower back and pelvis cause an aching feeling. Usually, this imbalance is temporary, and the dancer will grow out of it with time. Attending to correct pelvic alignment in dynamic movements and strengthening the abdominal muscles while stretching the backs of the legs and the front of the hips can help prevent the pain.

PRICED

When an injury occurs, jazz dancers need to know the steps to limit further harm. The PRICED method is a simple, easily remembered guide for immediate treatment of new injuries (see table 3.1; Sefcovic, 2010). The first step of the PRICED method is protection. **Protection** means that you remove additional danger or risk from the injured area. If an injury occurs, stop what you are doing and make sure that you move out of the way from further harm. This step may include protecting the

Table 3.1 PRICED

Protection	Remove additional danger or risk from the injured area.
Rest	Stop dancing and stop moving the injured area.
Ice	Apply ice to the injured area for 20 minutes every 2 hours.
Compression	Apply an elastic compression bandage, compression tights, or compression sleeve to the injured area.
Elevation	Raise the injured area above the heart.
Diagnosis	Acute injuries should be evaluated by a health care professional.

injured part by taking weight off it or supporting it in some way. If you cannot bear weight on an injured leg for at least three steps, seek medical attention.

After the injured body part is protected, the next step in the method is rest. **Rest** means that you stop dancing and stop moving the injured area. Continued stress on an injured body part can make things worse, causing further injury and delaying the healing process. Research now suggests, however, that stopping movement altogether may not be appropriate in all situations. In some cases, passive movement during rest is recommended to prevent the joint from becoming stiff and to aid in the healing process. The next step in the method is ice. **Ice** means that you apply ice to the injured area. Ice restricts the blood flow to the area, thus preventing excess swelling and discomfort. The recommendation is to apply ice for 20 minutes every 2 hours.

SAFETY TIP

Icing should not be done right before class because your body needs to be warm before beginning physical activity. If you have been icing, you should allow the skin to return to normal color and temperature before returning to activity. Better yet, you should warm it up before beginning class.

After the injury is protected, rested, and iced, the next step is compression. **Compression** means that you apply an elastic compression bandage, compression tights, or a compression sleeve to the injured area. Wrapping the injured part in an elastic bandage reduces swelling and helps support the injured part. Be careful not to make the elastic band too tight. A good guide is to allow room for two fingers to fit inside the wrap. After compression, the next step is elevation. **Elevation** means that you raise the body part above the heart to promote circulation and reduce inflammation. The final step of the method is diagnosis. There is no replacement for seeing a health care professional. If pain is severe or persists, seek medical attention.

Understanding your body, the way in which it moves, the importance of healthy posture, and the PRICED first-aid steps will not guarantee that you will avoid an injury, but it will greatly reduce the chance that you will have one and will increase the speed of recovery. With an appreciation of general studio safety, personal safety, and injury prevention, the next step is to look at nutrition.

NUTRITION, HYDRATION, AND REST

A dancer's primary tool is the body. A healthy body leads to progress and improvement as a dancer. In order to have a healthy body, you need the right amount of food, water, and rest.

Nutrition

When it comes to food, what you put into your body matters. Dancers work hard and need lots of fuel in the right combination of carbohydrate, fat, protein, vitamins, and minerals. Carbohydrate should make up about 55 to 60 percent of the food intake of the average dance student (Clarkson, 2003). Whole-grain bread, cereal, rice, and pasta are nutrient-dense complex carbohydrates that help dancers sustain energy during classes and rehearsals.

Fat is important for long rehearsals or classes in which the dancer is constantly moving for 20 minutes or longer. Fat should make up 20 to 30 percent of a dancer's food intake (Clarkson, 2003).

Protein helps rebuild muscle fibers that break down from physical exertion. Protein-rich foods that are low in fat include skinless turkey and chicken. For dancers who do not eat meat, tofu and beans make good protein sources. Protein should make up 12 to 15 percent of a dancer's food intake (Clarkson, 2003).

Minerals and vitamins are best received through a balanced diet rich in vegetables and fruits. Vitamin and mineral supplements should be approached carefully because they could do more harm than good if not taken in the right balance. In addition to consuming the proper amount of carbohydrate, fat, protein, vitamins, and minerals, a dancer needs to be well hydrated.

Hydration

Having plenty of liquids before and throughout a dance class is important. Dancers sweat, and sweat dehydrates the body. A dancer can lose up to two liters of water in a single dance class (Clarkson, 2003). Most teachers will let you bring a water bottle to class if you keep it safely off to the side. Take advantage of this practice and keep your body hydrated so that you can get the most from your dance class.

DID YOU KNOW?

Rethink your drink: Coffee drinks, soda, alcohol, and sugary beverages may be tempting, but they offer little or no nutrition and can even lead to dehydration. Replacing one or more of these drinks with water during the day will rehydrate you and reduce the number of empty calories you consume.

Rest

Dancers, especially young dancers, seldom realize the importance of proper rest. Your body needs time to recuperate from strenuous activity. You need to balance out physical exertion with downtime to reenergize. This pattern is called the exertion-recuperation cycle. A good night's sleep is sometimes the most important ingredient for a safe, productive, and enjoyable dance class.

SUMMARY

In this chapter you learned that safety starts with a studio space and floor that is clear of portable barres, chairs, dance bags, water bottles, and shoes and free of slick spots. You then learned that an awareness of your personal space helps avoid collisions and that sharing appropriate personal health information with your instructor can help in an emergency. Injury prevention starts with the space but also includes an understanding of the anatomy of your skeletal and muscular systems as well as kinesiology of how your joints move in planes of space. You discovered the PRICED method of first aid and learned the value of nutrition, water, and rest. You are ready for the next step. In the following chapter you will discover the best ways to approach learning and practicing jazz dance.

To find supplementary materials for this chapter, such as learning activities, e-journal assignments, and web links, visit the web resource at **www.HumanKinetics.com/BeginningJazzDance.**

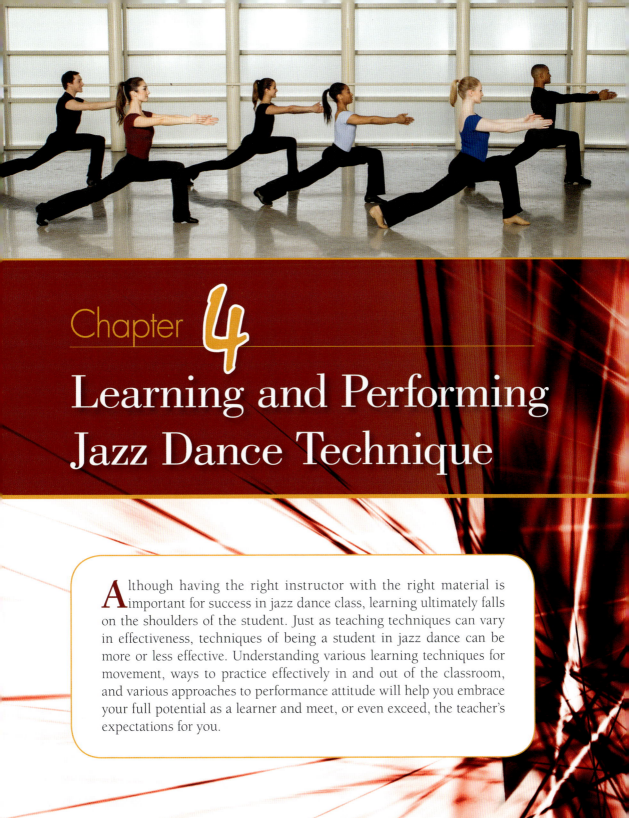

Chapter 4

Learning and Performing Jazz Dance Technique

Although having the right instructor with the right material is important for success in jazz dance class, learning ultimately falls on the shoulders of the student. Just as teaching techniques can vary in effectiveness, techniques of being a student in jazz dance can be more or less effective. Understanding various learning techniques for movement, ways to practice effectively in and out of the classroom, and various approaches to performance attitude will help you embrace your full potential as a learner and meet, or even exceed, the teacher's expectations for you.

LEARNING MOVEMENT TECHNIQUE

Your ability to learn movement technique is not just a natural ability to pick up steps that you are either born with or not. You can use learnable skills to make yourself a more effective student of dance. Having strong skills of movement observation, analysis, musicality, and rhythm opens your body and mind to the information presented in jazz dance class.

Simply being present in class will not lead to success in learning jazz dance. You must practice good observation skills. **Observation skills** include the three learning modalities: aural (listen), visual (watch), and kinesthetic (do). We all have different preferences. Some learn better from watching someone else do a step, whereas others learn best by getting up and doing it. You should understand your personal preference but also recognize that when you are open to all three learning modalities, you get the most out of your observational skills.

Listen

Listening to the teacher's instructions, what he or she says and how he or she says it, gives you your first window into the lesson or steps presented. Dance steps have a unique vocabulary. Listening to the vocabulary cues and knowing the names of steps helps you retrieve them easily from your memory, freeing up mental attention to focus on other details. **Vocabulary cues** are the names of steps and movement techniques used for instruction. Hearing the name of the steps or techniques along with the experience of doing them helps create a connection between your mind and body. If your mind commits the name of the step to memory while the body executes it, your body can more readily retrieve that step later when the teacher calls for it. The name of the step becomes a shortcut that allows your body quick access to an otherwise complex movement.

Besides learning the names of the steps, listening to the rhythm of the teacher's words and counts also brings important information to the learning process. **Rhythmic cues** are the patterned delivery of words or sounds to convey information about movement. Jazz dance is a rhythm-driven dance form, and teachers often use a rhythmic pattern in saying the steps to relay important details of how to do the step. Jazz teachers sometimes even scat nonsensical sounds ("Zwee-bop-ah-doo-dah") to express complex ideas. Having an ear for rhythm saves the tediously drawn-out explanation of movement rhythms that would be necessary if we could not express rhythms verbally.

The teacher's words convey information not only through rhythm but also through intonation. **Intonation cues** are the use of pitch in delivery of words or sounds to convey information about movement. The rise and fall of the tone of the teacher's voice suggests qualities of movement that you should use. Often, teachers use higher intonation to suggest moments of movement that are meant to be done high up on the toes or in leaps in the air and low intonation for steps meant to be done closer to the ground and with strong, weighty energy. Each teacher has a distinct personal style in delivering oral cues. Learning to listen carefully to the vocabulary, rhythmic, and intonation cues in jazz dance class assists you in getting the most out of the instruction and in developing observation skills that make you a more effective learner of movement.

Watch

Besides listening, watching the teacher or another student demonstrate movements gives you a direct frame of reference for what you are trying to accomplish. The first step in being able to watch the movement demonstration is to position yourself in the room where you can see clearly. This statement seems simplistic, but students often stand behind others and do not have a clear view of the person doing the demonstration. Perhaps out of a sense of politeness or not wanting to draw attention, they refrain from moving into a position where they can see clearly. You deserve to get the most out of your class. Being able to watch the step demonstrated is an important part of the learning process.

After you are positioned to see the demonstration, learn to look for both the whole picture and the details. Seeing the whole picture lets you see how all the parts of the body work together and how they relate to one another. Seeing the details helps you ascertain the specific elements of execution needed. The skill of zooming your focus out, seeing the entire body in coordination, and zooming your focus in, seeing the specific details, helps you get a complete sense of the movement technique being taught. Stuck in one type of focus, your observation of the movement will lead to only partial understanding. With practice, your ability to adjust your focus to see the whole picture and the details will improve.

Do

Listening and watching alone are not enough. Dance is about movement, and dancers learn from moving their bodies. You can stand around, listen to a description of the step, and watch it demonstrated for hours and still not get the experience you would gain from simply doing the step. Although listening and watching help you process the movement mentally, actually doing the step physically involves bodily learning.

A tool that helps students bodily learn is to shadow the teacher. You should do this unless a teacher specifically asks you to stand still and listen or watch. Dancers who shadow the teacher's demonstration or instruction assimilate the information into their bodies faster. The most eager and focused students in a

ACTIVITY

LISTEN, WATCH, DO

Try this with a partner. Partner A describes a movement using voice only. Partner B executes it. Next, partner A silently demonstrates a different movement, while partner B watches. Partner B executes it. Then, partner A silently demonstrates a movement, while partner B shadows partner A. Finally, put all three together. Partner A describes while demonstrating, and partner B listens, watches, and shadows partner A. Which works best for you?

class are often the ones who are shadowing the teacher's every move. While others stand still and listen or watch, students who shadow while simultaneously listening and watching tend to be the best prepared when it is time to do the movement themselves. If you set your goals as a student to practice the observational skills of listening, watching, and doing, you will soak up the information presented in class and put yourself in the best position to learn.

ANALYZING MOVEMENT SKILLS

Sharp observation skills bring in information that, coupled with good analyzing skills, can turn into success in the jazz dance class. The ability to analyze the movement based on its shape, use of space, use of time, use of energy, weight, and effort actions, makes for exciting and dynamic jazz dance.

Body Shape

Body shape is the overall structure of the body during a single step or string of steps. You can analyze the body shape of a single step or string of steps by observing

- what body parts are in motion,
- how it initiates,
- how it sequences,
- how it displays connection within the body, and
- how it follows through or transitions.

Body Parts

Being clear on what body parts are in motion helps clarify movement. When the teacher demonstrates a step that includes footwork accompanied by a motion with the right hand, you should use just those body parts—the feet and the right hand. Adding movement of the left arm and a hip, when not called for, makes the step unclear. The key to analyzing body parts and their shape in movement is to be specific. The more specific you are, the greater the success you will have. After you see clearly which body part or parts are in motion, the next step is to analyze how it begins.

Initiation

How a movement initiates is important. **Initiation** is how the movement begins. **Inner initiation** occurs when movement begins from a central point in the body and moves outward. An example would be moving the right shoulder forward and then following the flow of energy out the right arm and through the fingers. Inner-initiated movement is often self-expressive, relating an inner emotion to the outside world.

    Outer initiation occurs when movement begins from the outer edges of the body or from the environment and moves toward the center. An example would be moving the fingertips then following the energy through the arm and into the chest. Outer-initiated movement often displays a sense of outside forces acting on you.

Simultaneous initiation occurs when body parts all begin moving at once. For example, when you begin a jumping jack, both arms and both legs move at the same time. Simultaneously initiated movement often expresses control over the body, either the ease and coordination of your having control of your body or, in contrast, the robot-like rigidity of your body controlled by another. Now that you have determined what specific body parts are involved and whether they begin with inner, outer, or simultaneous initiation, the next step is to look at the sequence.

> **ACTIVITY**
>
> ### INITIATION EXPLORATION
>
> Start with your arms at your side. The goal is to end with them over your head. First, use inner initiation by starting from your shoulder and then working through your elbow and out to your fingertips to raise the arm. Then, reset and use outer initiation by starting from your fingertips and then working through your elbow and finally to your shoulder to raise the arm. Finally, reset and then raise the arm as a whole unit using simultaneous initiation.

Sequence

Sequence is the order in which movements occur. We can describe the sequencing of movement through the body in three ways: sequential, successive, and simultaneous.

Sequential sequence happens when movement follows one after the other in nonadjacent body parts. If you raise your right shoulder up to your ear and then replace it, and then do the same with your left shoulder, you are using sequential sequencing. Sequential sequencing often results in fragmented, disjointed movement.

Successive sequence happens when movement follows one after the other in adjacent body parts. If you raise your right shoulder to your ear and then let that movement flow into your right arm by lifting the right elbow and continuing into the right wrist, you are using successive sequencing. Successive sequencing often results in naturally flowing movement.

Simultaneous sequence happens when movements occur at the same time. If you raise both shoulders to your ears and then replace them at precisely the same time, you are using simultaneous sequencing. By understanding which body parts move, how they initiate, and how they sequence, you can now look at their connectivity.

Connectivity

Connectivity is the pattern of relationship between body parts. Six patterns of connectivity were discussed earlier in chapter 2: breath, core-distal, head-tail, upper-lower, body-half, and cross lateral. Seeing how the movement relates to other parts of the body through movement patterns of connectivity serves as a shortcut for understanding complex movement. After determining which body parts move, how they initiate, how they sequence, and how they connect to the rest of the body, you can take the final step in analyzing the form of the steps presented in class by analyzing the follow-through.

Follow-Through

Follow-through is the residual movement after the main action. For example, when you throw a ball, your arm does not stop the moment the ball leaves your hand. Rather, your arm follows through to complete the arcing motion that it started. Jazz dance steps have a follow-through as well. A **transition** is a follow-through that connects one movement to the next. If you execute just the main actions and forget the follow-throughs or transitions, your movement quality will likely appear choppy and awkward.

Two common types of transitions are shifting and transformational. In a **shifting transition**, the movement changes abruptly from one step to the next. Shift transitions in dance resemble the quick cuts in a movie action scene. They are common in street jazz and hip-hop-influenced jazz dance styles.

In a **transformational transition**, one step gradually evolves into the following one, blurring the line between the beginnings and endings of each step. Transformational transitions in dance look like subtle cross fades in a movie or video that you barely notice. They are common in contemporary jazz dance.

Looking at and analyzing a dance step by its form (body part, initiation, sequence, connectivity, and follow-through or transition) will help you learn and perform the overall shape of the steps. Another way to analyze and learn movement is to look at how the dance step or combination uses space.

Use of Space

The use of space focuses on the relationship between the shape of your body, the pathway it takes, and the focus of your attention. Shape, pathway, and focus can be either direct or indirect. Keep in mind that you can analyze space in dance in various ways.

Choreographers, people who make up dances, refer to space in compositional terms using a variety of elements such as level, direction, dimension, and so on. In this case, we are focusing specifically on your use of personal space while analyzing and learning movement. Do not be confused by the overlapping terminology between compositional space and personal space. For now, we focus on personal space.

Direct space is a specific and exact use of shape, pathway, and focus. **Indirect space** is a nonspecific and general use of shape, pathway, and focus. **Shape** is the position of the body in space. Sometimes, a teacher will demonstrate a step with the arm and body ending in an exact position (direct space). Other times, a teacher will tell you to place your arm generally to the side (indirect space). These are contrasting uses of direct and indirect shape.

Pathways can be direct or indirect as well. **Pathway** is the route that the body takes between shapes. Performing an arm movement that starts with your right hand touching your left shoulder, slices across your chest to the right shoulder, and extends the right elbow, keeping the arm parallel to the floor until it is fully extended, uses a direct pathway. In contrast, starting from that same position and throwing the arm out to the side in a slashing motion uses an indirect pathway. Steps can also transition from one spatial relationship to the other. A movement that begins direct can grow increasingly indirect, and a movement that begins indirect can grow increasingly direct.

Focus is the orientation of attention to the surrounding space. Think of focus as one of three states: gas, liquid, or solid. When you focus directly on one specific point in space and have tunnel vision, your focus is a solid state. When you focus indirectly, taking in everything within your field of vision, including things on the periphery, your focus is a gas state. When your focus is direct but flows from one specific point to another, it is a liquid state.

The combination of direct and indirect shape, pathway, and focus brings variety and specificity to understanding the use of space in learning dance. The ability to differentiate the use of direct and indirect space on a demonstrated step helps you understand what the teacher expects. Applying all of these at one time can be overwhelming, so you might focus on just one at a time. For example, tell yourself that the next time the teacher demonstrates the step, you will pay attention to the use of space in regard to focus. After you feel confident with that, go on to another element. With time and practice, you will become fluent in picking up spatial relationships and improve your ability to learn movement. In addition to analyzing form and the use of space, an understanding of the use of time aids in learning movement.

Use of Time

The use of time is either quick or sustained. But do not confuse quick and sustained movements with fast and slow tempos. Quick movement is often done at a fast tempo, and sustained movement can be certainly done at a slow tempo, but that is not necessarily so. If you perform a step at a slow pace (tempo) but with sudden, jerky, staccato movement, you display quick use of time. On the contrary, if you execute a step at a fast tempo but with smooth, luxurious, legato movement, you display sustained use of time.

You can also perform movement that transitions from quick to sustained or from slow to fast and vice versa. Decreasing or accelerating tempo creates striking effects while dancing. In jazz dance class, watch for the tempo and timing of the steps but do not forget to observe the use of time within those tempos. Your ability to analyze the differences between use of time and tempo not only helps you learn movement with more detail but also makes you a more interesting dancer to watch. Along with the use of space and use of time, the use of weight plays a major role in jazz dance.

Use of Weight

Use of weight describes whether you use strong or light muscular energy when moving. Jazz dance, known for its energy and vitality, commonly uses a lot of weight. When you reach your arm up above your head, your use of weight makes a huge difference. A strong use of weight, engaging the muscles and forcefully hitting the position overhead, displays great energy. A light use of weight, effortlessly lifting and placing the arm overhead, displays easy, relaxed energy.

Increasing or decreasing weight also creates movement that varies in its use of strength rather than maintains the same relationship to weight. Moving from light weight to strong weight (increasing pressure) shows a building tension as the relaxed muscles of the body contract, becoming more engaged and forceful. Moving from strong weight to light weight (decreasing pressure) displays a releasing of tension as the engaged muscles of the body relax, becoming more effortless. Although jazz dance may stereotypically embrace strong weight or energy, your versatility to analyze and use strong weight, light weight, decreasing pressure, and increasing pressure will make you an exciting dancer. Furthermore, combining the elements of space, time, and weight leads you to discover effort actions, which make movement come to life.

Effort Actions

If you played the piano and could play complex rhythms but could use only one key, your performance would be boring. The same goes with dance. If you do all the steps in complex rhythms but can hit only one note, you get bored. Dance comprises eight effort actions that create a dynamic scale for movement, much as the keys of a piano make a scale. **Effort actions** come from the combination of one element of space (either direct or indirect) with one element of time (quick or sustained) and one element of weight (strong or light). Eight combinations exist, making up the eight effort actions (see table 4.1). Each of the effort actions has a name that serves as a shortcut to access the combination of elements.

Table 4.1 Effort Actions

Effort action	Space	Time	Weight
Punch	Direct	Quick	Strong
Dab	Direct	Quick	Light
Glide	Direct	Sustained	Light
Press	Direct	Sustained	Strong
Slash	Indirect	Quick	Strong
Flick	Indirect	Quick	Light
Float	Indirect	Sustained	Light
Wring	Indirect	Sustained	Strong

In the punch effort action, you move with direct space, quick time, and strong weight. Punching actions abound in the work of drill teams and cheerleaders. Because they strive for unison, they use direct space and quick time. Indirect space is not unison by definition, and sustained time would expose every little mistake. Strong weight makes the movement energetic.

In the dab effort action, you move with direct space, quick time, but light weight. Dabbing occurs when you tap on your mobile device.

In the glide effort action, you move with direct space, sustained time, and light weight, like a skater sailing across the ice on one foot.

In the press effort action, you move with direct space, sustained time, and strong weight, like someone pushing a piano across the room.

In the slash effort action, you move with indirect space, quick time, and strong weight. Slashing movement resembles that of a lion tamer brandishing a whip.

In the flick effort action, you move with indirect space, quick time, and light weight, like shooing away a fly.

In the float effort action, you move with indirect space, sustained time, and light weight, as if you are a feather or bubble tossed about by the wind.

In the wring effort action, you move with indirect space, sustained time, and strong weight, similar to the feeling of wringing the water out of a dishcloth or towel.

The skill to analyze the movement presented in jazz dance class by its effort action clarifies the quality of the dance movements and adds to the base of skills you have at your disposal. With practice, you will become a stronger, better student of dance by applying the analyzing skills discussed here. Your ability to analyze form (the body parts, initiation, sequence, connection, and follow-through), use of space (direct or indirect), use of time (quick or sustained), use of weight (strong or light), and the eight effort actions (punch, dab, glide, press, slash, flick, float, wring) will grow in time and increase not only your skill but also, and more importantly, your enjoyment. Because the roots of jazz dance closely connect to music, next you need to learn ways to increase your musicality and rhythmic skills.

HONING MUSICALITY AND RHYTHMIC SKILLS

Because early jazz dance and jazz music existed as one entity (much like hip-hop in contemporary culture) and because today popular music often accompanies jazz dance, jazz dancers need musicality and rhythmic skills. Rhythmic skills, such as the ability to count music, to understand rhythmic phrasing, and to use syncopation, are vital for the jazz dance student.

Counting Music

Jazz dancers count music differently than musicians do. Whereas musicians count in measures, dancers count in phrases. The most common phrase of music used in jazz dance class consists of eight beats. A **beat** is the regularly occurring pulse of the music. The second most common phrase in jazz dance class consists of six beats. Jazz dancers break the beats themselves into smaller parts. When you divide the basic beat into two parts, you use duple meter. Instead of counting only the beat, you add "and" between the counts. Figure 4.1 is an example of a four-beat phrase in regular and duple meter.

Figure 4.1 Regular and duple meter.

In triple meter, you divide the basic beat into three parts and add "and uh" between each count (see figure 4.2).

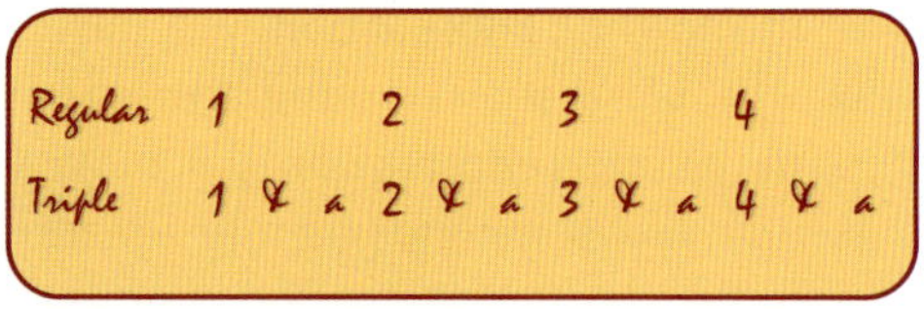

Less commonly, jazz dancers divide the beat further into four parts to make quadruple meter. In this case, the counts between the beat are pronounced "ee and uh" (see figure 4.3).

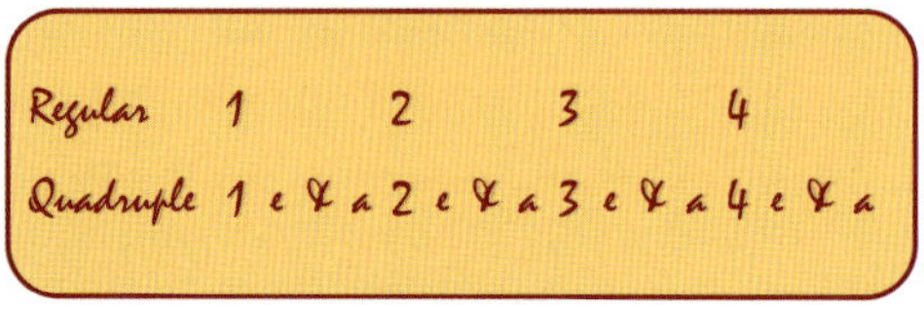

Figure 4.2 Triple meter.

Your ability to count the music and to differentiate between duple and triple meter will aid the learning process in class and prepare you to explore more complex rhythmic phrasing.

Rhythmic Phrasing

Figure 4.3 Quadruple meter.

Keeping the beat is important, but slavishly sticking to it gets dull. In rhythmic phrasing for jazz dance, the difference between being on top of the beat, in the belly of the beat, and in the pocket makes your phrasing unique and musical. When dancing strictly to the beat of the music without variation, a dancer is in the belly of the beat. The dancer is keeping an almost metronome-like consistency. Although you should prefer keeping the beat to not keeping the beat, nuanced variations create more musically interesting rhythmic movement.

Being on top of the beat happens when you anticipate the beat slightly, attacking it right as the downbeat hits. This action appears almost ahead of the beat, but not really, and it creates a dynamic visual accent. Of course, too much on top of the beat looks anxious and unsettling.

Being in the pocket, by being almost behind the beat, just slipping it in before the next beat comes, creates a relaxed, cool effect and adds an element of surprise. Varying your phrasing by dancing occasionally on top of the beat and in the pocket as opposed to dancing only in the belly of the beat expresses aliveness and vitality through dance. After you are given the counts in jazz dance class, try exploring different rhythmic phrasings to make the steps your own.

ACTIVITY

RHYTHMIC PHRASING

Play a favorite piece of music with a strong rhythm. Practice clapping on top of the beat first. Then, clap in the pocket. Finally, clap in the belly of the beat.

Syncopation

Syncopation is the placing of an accent unexpectedly on the upbeat rather than the downbeat. In musical phrases of eight or six beats, as commonly found in jazz dance class, syncopation means the even counts receive the emphasis. When subdividing the beat in duple meter, the emphasis falls on the "ands." In triple and quadruple meter, the emphasis occurs on the "uhs" (see figure 4.4).

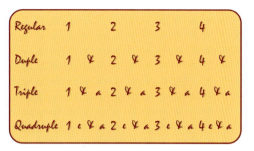

Figure 4.4   Syncopation.

An effective way to understand syncopation for jazz dance involves duple and triple meter. For syncopation, you use the triple meter, but leave out the "and" count (see figure 4.5).

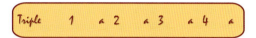

Figure 4.5   Counting syncopation.

Try clapping this rhythm to help clarify it. First, clap the duple rhythm: 1 and 2, 3 and 4. Then, clap the syncopated rhythm using triple meter: 1 a 2, 3 a 4. Syncopating the rhythm creates excitement. The duple meter rhythm gets dull and predictable where syncopation makes the step swing.

With a rhythm-driven dance form such as jazz, you learn to be not only a dancer but also a musician of the body. The ability to count music, phrase rhythmically, and use syncopation makes jazz dancers particularly exciting movers. While learning exercises in class, draw your awareness to the aspects of musicality and rhythmic skills discussed here to help you understand the nuances of the movement and discover your own expression through rhythm.

By practicing your observational, analytical, musical, and rhythmic skills in jazz dance class, your ability to learn movement technique will grow. You will become more effective at memorizing steps, exercises, and combinations. The stronger you become and the more effective you are at assimilating movement material, the more enjoyment you will get from your class experience when it comes time to perform in class.

ENHANCING PERFORMANCE IN CLASS

Besides identifying helpful learning skills, sport psychology and related fields have discovered important habits that enhance classroom performance. By engaging the habits of deliberate practice, finding flow, and the feedback loop, you can grow as both a dancer and a learner.

Deliberate Practice

Deliberate practice is working on technique just beyond your grasp, seeking constant critical feedback, and focusing on strengthening weaknesses (Ericsson, 2006).

In order to perform this complex coordination exercise that combines the single forced-arch leg isolation with the stagger arm combination, dancers engage deliberate practice and constantly seek critical feedback from the teacher.

Just showing up to class and going through the motions is not enough. You must fully engage what you are doing. Specific earmarks of deliberate practice separate it from just ordinary practice.

Working on technique just beyond your grasp means that you challenge yourself. A gap should separate what you are able to do and what you try to do. Simply going over what you can do comfortably does not lead to growth. You may look good to those around you if you always stay within your comfort zone, but only as long as the zone in class remains stagnant. To grow, you have to work on skills just beyond your grasp. Although the teacher may encourage you in this direction, ultimately only you can decide to try something different, difficult, and beyond your grasp. This habit is important for increasing performance in class.

The second habit of deliberate practice, seeking constant critical feedback, means that you actively search for corrections. The student who hides in the back to avoid being seen, asks for feedback only from friends who tend to deliver compliments, and reacts to critical feedback as a personal attack misses the opportunity to learn and improve. To seek constant critical feedback, you must put yourself forward to be seen, ask for feedback from peers who will give you honest and constructive comments, and embrace each bit of critical feedback as a gift.

The third habit of deliberate practice, focusing on strengthening weaknesses, means that you work on your deficient skill areas to improve them rather than spend your time working only on what you already do well. Sometimes dancers who do not understand this habit only take classes in which they perform well or from teachers who give them only positive feedback. But directing attention and effort toward strengthening your weaknesses creates the greatest improvement. To develop the three habits of deliberate practice, here are three useful tools to explore.

Attentive Repetition

Attentive repetition means working with full mental focus on a skill repeatedly by finding deeper layers of challenge. **Marking** means to do a movement or step with reserved energy and use of space. Sometimes, the temptation to mark through the steps and exercises, especially when you perform them repeatedly and feel comfortable with the skill, leads dancers to execute the skill halfheartedly. When you practice a skill halfheartedly, you improve at doing it halfheartedly, not at doing it fully. Marking, like a marching band moving in place, means to move your feet and make no progress. Mindlessly repeating dance steps and exercises does little to help you learn. Instead, develop the passion to master, the desire to focus and find new details and challenges within what you already know. Do not let yourself settle for an approximation of the skill. Strive to master it.

Feel It From Inside

Another quick tool, **feel it from inside**, is a process that includes setting a goal, reaching for it, evaluating the attempt, and repeating the cycle (Coyle, 2009). Set a clear goal, such as learning a new dance step, by visualizing it with detail and committing to it. Then, reach for it by trying, giving it your best effort. The next part is vital: Evaluate the gap between the goal and your attempt. Look at all the details of the gap. Finally, repeat the cycle. Avoid the pitfalls of not having a clear goal in mind, not visualizing it with detail, not attempting to reach for the goal with full effort, not critically evaluating the difference between your goal and your attempt, and not trying again. You probably recognize when you have successfully used this process in the past without being conscious of it. You also might recognize times when one of the pitfalls became an obstacle. Using this tool as a quick guide, you can have greater success in class performance.

The three habits and three tools of deliberate practice lead to greater performance in the jazz dance class. Try them and see which work best for your personal learning style. Deliberate practice also goes hand in hand with finding flow.

ACTIVITY

FEEL IT FROM INSIDE

In the process of learning a new movement, try this four-step process:

1. Visualize it.
2. Do it.
3. Evaluate the gap.
4. Do it again.

Finding Flow

Flow is a state of optimal inner experience, characterized by absorption in the moment from the merging of action and awareness (Czikszentmihalyi, 1990). In sport, the phrase "in the zone" refers to being in a state of flow. Dancers often experience this state of complete absorption. Most of the time, it happens accidentally, but you can take certain steps to help bring it about. First, flow needs a challenge that takes skill with the possibility, not the certainty, of control. You need to challenge yourself, to find your edge. Your edge is that place where you may do it, but you may also fail. If you stay too far from the edge, you never reach or grow. If you go too far over the edge, you end up frustrated and give up quickly. If you never make mistakes, you are working within your comfort zone. Making mistakes is not a problem; instead, it is an important sign that you are learning.

Achieving flow also requires complete concentration on the task. Our culture promotes multitasking as an important skill, but the diverted focus of multitasking does not lead to effective learning or states of flow. Practicing multitasking makes you better at multitasking, but not any particular skill. Performing an exercise in jazz dance class while going over your homework assignments for the evening will sap you of your ability to learn the skill you are currently working on and keep you from feeling that experience of being in the zone, or in flow. In flow, your actions and your awareness merge. It is the opposite of multitasking.

DID YOU KNOW?

Olympic athletes hire sport psychologists and use their techniques when preparing to compete. Athletes with their headphones on and eyes closed are likely using some of the techniques listed earlier to enhance performance. Dancers and athletes use many of the same practices in training and preparation.

From the challenges of working at your edge and the complete absorption of action and awareness, flow creates an experience of effortless, timeless loss of self-consciousness. As soon as you become aware that you are experiencing a state of flow, you have lost it. But if you develop the habits of finding your edge and focusing on the task, you increase your chances of accessing a state of flow.

Feedback Loop

A dance class includes a number of feedback loops. The secret to getting the most out of your learning experience is to engage as many of them as possible and as often as you can. Feedback loops exist between you and the teacher, yourself, and the mirror.

Feedback From the Teacher

Feedback from the teacher exists in many ways. It can come in the form of oral, visual, and physical cues. You might be most familiar with oral feedback, when the teachers says, "Good job" or suggests a correction: "Try it again, but this time with more energy." Visual feedback can come in the form of a smile, a shake of the head, or a thumb-up gesture. Physical feedback comes from hands-on corrections that possibly correct your posture or remind you where to focus while executing a step. Awareness of all the oral, visual, and physical feedback that the teacher delivers helps you gather information from which to learn.

Feedback From Self

The majority of feedback you find in a jazz dance class comes from yourself. In the simplest form of self-feedback, when you trip or make a mistake, your body tells you that something did not go right. In that moment of a mistake, if you can avoid the tendency to judge yourself negatively and instead accept the information as helpful, you can turn each moment into a feedback loop. For example, you attempt to do a turnaround yourself, but each time you fall to your right side. Instead of getting frustrated, use the feedback that you are going off balance to the right to correct your next attempt at the turn.

Another form of self-feedback is kinesthetic sensing. Kinesthetic sensing is the ability to feel the position of your body and limbs in space. When you imitate a position or step that the teacher demonstrates, you can sense whether you feel you have hit the right position. Dancers develop the ability to sense their position in space kinesthetically and make adjustments based on that feeling. With practice, your ability to use kinesthetic sensing will grow.

Feedback From the Mirror

As a skill, kinesthetic sensing takes time to develop, so dancers often use a mirror. The mirror gives you vital feedback to let you know that the shape you make or the step you execute looks the way you want it to look. The mirror serves as an important feedback tool in the jazz dance class. But if you rely too heavily on information coming to you from the mirror, you may forget to develop your kinesthetic sense. The tool becomes a crutch. You will not always be able to look in the mirror for feedback, so you need to strike a balance between kinesthetic sense and mirror feedback.

The benefits from the habits of deliberate practice, finding flow, and the feedback loop go beyond the jazz dance class. These habits apply to any endeavor, whether another type of dance, another physical skill such as a sport, or study in a classroom. Although these habits are not specific to jazz dance, they will greatly increase your performance in jazz dance class.

DEVELOPING A PERFORMANCE ATTITUDE

You may not intend to perform on a stage, but jazz dance does develop performance skills. Performance attitude in the jazz dance class focuses on developing expression, ensemble skills, and artistic interpretation. All of these come into play, whether performing a combination in the studio or on a stage.

Expression

Jazz dance is an expressive art form. The ability to be naturally expressive, to use your whole body, and to connect directly with others make jazz dance entertaining and joyful. The combination at the end of a jazz dance class gives an excellent opportunity to develop expression, but you can apply it to all of jazz dance class, beginning with the first exercise.

Natural Expression

Jazz dance expresses a wide array of emotions including joy, sorrow, sensuality, angst, and humor. To make the performance of these large, powerful emotions expressive to others, they need to be natural and organic. Mugging is making over-exaggerated facial expressions. To express naturally and avoid mugging, make sure that you feel the emotions from the inside. Doing this may take practice, especially when you first learn a step or combination and need to marshal all your concentration to do the step. But practicing natural expression from the beginning, alongside learning the physical aspects of the steps, helps to imprint in your body and mind that expression and physical movement go together. Practicing one without the other only reduces your ability to connect the two.

Whole-Body Expressivity

Just as you should not disconnect your facial expressions from your body, you should also make sure that your whole body expresses what your face does. An expression of joy on your face, such as a smile, permeates throughout the entire body, creating lightness and radiant energy in the torso and limbs. An expression of angst on your face, such as furrowing your brow, also permeates through your body, perhaps creating tension in the muscles of your shoulders, hands, and abdomen. Whole-body expressivity aids in natural expression, and natural expression aids in whole-body expressivity. The mind and body are a two-way street.

Directly Expressive

Jazz dance is a directly expressive dance form. You connect, often through eye contact, with those around you, whether they are dancing along with you or watching from the front and sides. If you learn jazz dance steps with an inward focus, when it comes time to execute them you will focus inward and find direct expression an added hurdle.

Natural expression, whole-body expression, and being directly expressive should be learned along with the technical aspects of the steps and combinations. A dancer who spends time perfecting technical execution of the steps at the cost of learning expressiveness will likely lack performance attitude. Because jazz dance is an expressive dance form, awareness of natural expression, whole-body expressivity, and being directly expressive is vital.

Ensemble Skills

Jazz dance classes happen in groups and therefore require the development of important ensemble skills. Spacing and flocking are skills that will make class more enjoyable and help you grow as a student of jazz dance.

Spacing

Spacing is the position within a group that a dancer must maintain, requiring an understanding of personal space as it relates to general space. In class, you learn not only exercises, steps, and combinations but also spacing in relationship to the dancers around you. For example, you may be the center of a group of three dancers. As you execute the steps, good spacing requires that you stay centered in the middle of the two other dancers and not get too close to one or the other. Like birds that fly in formation or fish that seemingly turn together on a dime, you will develop a sense of the space around you and adjust the size of your movement to maintain proper spacing. This task can be challenging when dancers do steps at varying sizes, but having good spacing skills means that you learn to be flexible and adapt to those around you using your peripheral vision. Spacing goes hand in hand with flocking.

Flocking

Flocking is the ability to adapt your movement spontaneously while also maintaining spacing. Flocking requires you to adjust the shapes and qualities of the steps. If you notice that everyone in the ensemble has one arm raised just a little higher than yours, you automatically make the adjustment. If you notice that everyone in the ensemble uses more light energy when kicking the leg to the side, you adjust to that. If you notice that the ensemble performs a head movement on count 2 and you do it on 3, you change to 2. When everyone in the ensemble learns the skill of flocking, cohesion develops so that the group resembles a flock of birds or a school of fish. Instead of operating like a group of soloists performing at the same time, a true sense of ensemble or oneness comes from the group, even when the movement does not require unison.

> ### ACTIVITY
>
> #### FLOCKING
>
> In a group of four people, stand so that you make a diamond and all face the same direction. The person at the point moves slowly and the other three follow exactly, imitating every detail like a flock of birds in flight. If the point person changes direction, the person in the diamond who is in front becomes the new leader. Continue practicing changing leaders without allowing gaps in the movement.

The ensemble skills of spacing and flocking create a sense of community among those in jazz dance class. Jazz dance began as a social dance form, and this aspect keeps that tradition alive. In our contemporary culture, which rewards fragmentation through competition, jazz dance offers a chance to reconnect and experience the joys of moving as part of a greater whole.

Artistic Interpretation

Artistic interpretation is the individual's personal creative expression of the movement. Jazz dance developed from people expressing themselves in social dance situations. Individual style continues to be an important element of jazz dance class. Although the teacher will ask you to learn the steps in a certain way, you will also be prompted to make the movement your own. As a jazz dance student, you want to find the balance between doing the steps properly and doing them with your own flair. Although rules are made to be broken, you must know what they are before you break them.

Your performance attitude in class consists of your ability to be expressive, to incorporate ensemble skills, and to add your own artistic interpretation. Work hard to learn the technical steps but also remember to enjoy natural whole-body expressivity, the sense of community from working as an ensemble, and the personal artistic interpretation that only you, as a unique individual, can bring to the class.

SUMMARY

Learning and performing jazz dance technique teaches much more than just the acquisition of steps. In developing observational, analytical, musical, and rhythmic skills, you learn to be a sharper, more insightful learner. In exploring the emerging habits from deliberate practice, finding flow, and engaging feedback, you open your mind and body to growth in class performance. In strengthening your expressive, ensemble, and artistic skills, you experience the joy of jazz dance. Take these skills with you as you begin to learn the basic positions of jazz dance and remember to return to them often.

To find supplementary materials for this chapter, such as learning activities, e-journal assignments, and web links, visit the web resource at **www.HumanKinetics.com/BeginningJazzDance.**

 **WEB RESOURCE** ▶

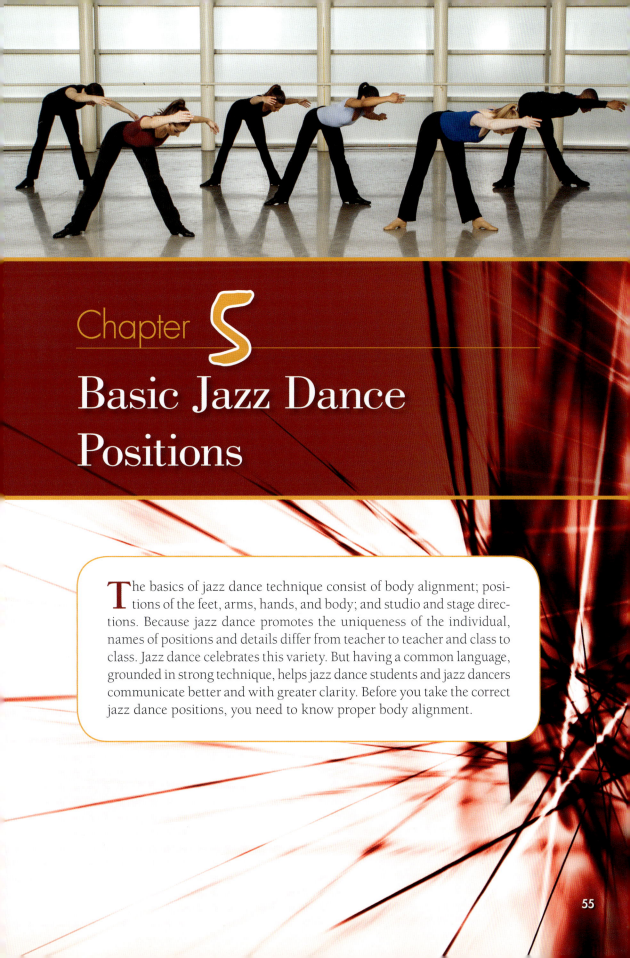

Chapter 5

Basic Jazz Dance Positions

The basics of jazz dance technique consist of body alignment; positions of the feet, arms, hands, and body; and studio and stage directions. Because jazz dance promotes the uniqueness of the individual, names of positions and details differ from teacher to teacher and class to class. Jazz dance celebrates this variety. But having a common language, grounded in strong technique, helps jazz dance students and jazz dancers communicate better and with greater clarity. Before you take the correct jazz dance positions, you need to know proper body alignment.

BODY ALIGNMENT

Alignment is the organization of body parts in relationship to each other. Figure 5.1 shows correct vertical alignment. In jazz dance, as well as other dance genres, proper alignment creates prolonged health and greater efficiency. The alignment of your ankles, knees, hips, and spine greatly affects the movement of your body. If the muscles supporting the ankles, knees, hips, and spine are weak or unbalanced, your posture will be poor, which will lead to uncoordinated movement and possibly injury.

Ankles

Your ankles are complex joints that can move in multiple directions (see figure 5.2). This range of movement gives your ankles the ability to function in helpful ways but also makes them susceptible to alignment issues such as pronation and supination. **Pronation** occurs when the ankles roll in toward the centerline of the body. This leads to an imbalance in which the inside of the ankle is weak and often too flexible while the outside is tight. Often known in dance class as rolling in, ankle pronation causes stress on the knees and often leads to ankle sprains on the inside of the ankle. **Supination** occurs when the ankles roll out from the centerline of the body. This leads to an imbalance in which the outside of the ankle is too flexible and the inside is tight. In dance class, this leads to what is often called sickling of the foot in the air and can lead to sprains on the outside of the foot when the dancer lands improperly. Proper ankle alignment keeps the foot healthy and relieves stress on the knees.

Figure 5.1   Correct vertical alignment.

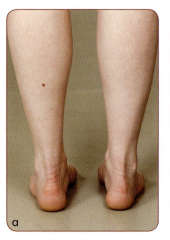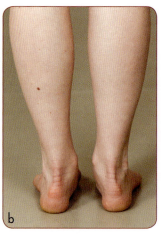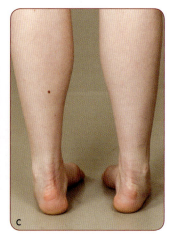

Figure 5.2   Ankles correctly aligned *(a)*, pronated *(b)*, and supinated *(c)*.

Knees

Your knees are hinge joints that primarily provide flexion and extension. Two important rules apply to the knees for dancing. The first rule is that the knees should always track over the first two toes when bending. If your knee tracks inside your foot, toward the centerline of your body, pronation of the ankle as well as stress on the inside of the knee may occur. If your knee tracks outside the foot, supination of the ankle and stress on the outside of the knee may occur.

The second important rule is to avoid going into hyperextension on a weight-bearing leg. In extension of the knee, the knee is straight. Some people have hypermobility in the knee and are able to go beyond a straight position into hyperextension. **Hyperextension** is the ability of a joint to go beyond extension. Dancers often call this locking the knees or swayback knees. If a knee is hyperextended and bearing weight, the muscles, tendons, and ligaments surrounding the knee can be harmed.

Besides serving as a base of support for all standing positions, a dancer's knees help create height in jumps and cushion the body, like shock absorbers, when landing. In jazz dance, movements are sometimes done on the floor on the knees. Healthy and mindful use of your knees keeps you dancing safely and with a smile on your face. Always pay close attention to how the knees function in relationship to the ankles in static positions and when moving. In addition to the close relationship between alignment of the ankles and knees, the alignment of the hips is an important factor in moving efficiently in dance.

> ## SAFETY TIP
>
> The rule to keep the knees over the toes is one of the most important rules for preventing injury. Any time your knees bend with weight on them, make sure to follow the knees-over-toes rule.

Hips

Proper alignment of your hips is central to jazz dance. Your hips are where your legs connect to your pelvis and your pelvis connects to your spine. A complex group of muscles works to make this area function properly, and any misalignment can adversely affect your overall alignment. Generally, you should center your hips over your knees and feet, tilting neither forward nor back. But you need to keep in mind exceptions to the rule. Although jazz dance forms influenced by ballet and modern techniques often follow the alignment mentioned before, jazz dance forms largely influenced by West African dance use the hips with a greater degree of forward tilt. Depending on the style of your teacher, you may experience either approach. For the purposes of the work described here, you will focus on the centered use of the hips and avoidance of the three most common misalignments.

The first common misalignment consists of sinking into one hip. **Sinking hip** occurs when the pelvis moves off center and body weight shifts more toward one side. Sinking hip is especially evident when you lift one leg off the floor. Avoid the tendency to sink into the hip of the leg that holds your weight.

The second common misalignment is forward pelvic tilt. In **forward pelvic tilt**, the top of the pelvis moves forward of the centerline of the body while the bottom of the pelvis moves behind the centerline of the body. Think of the pelvis as a bucket full of water. In forward tilt, the water spills out onto the ground in front of you. The opposite of forward pelvic tilt, **tucking under** is a third common hip misalignment in which the bottom of the pelvis rounds forward and under. This tense position affects the ability of the lower spine to move freely.

Proper alignment of the hips includes centering from side to side and from front to back and keeping the weight squarely over the knees and ankles. Misalignment affects not only the knees and ankles below but also the spine above.

Spine

Your spine consists of 33 bones, called vertebrae, that allow a variety of movement. The upper 24 are articulating and separated from each other by intervertebral discs, and the lower 9 are fused. The articulating vertebrae comprise three main sections, each with distinct movement capabilities, natural curves, and common postural issues. The spinal curves occur as primary or secondary curves. **Primary curves** are concave, hollowing out toward the front of the body. Curling up into a ball, like in the fetal position, is a full-body primary curve. **Secondary curves** are convex, bulging out toward the front of the body. If you imagine a gymnast bending backward to place the hands on the floor behind her or him, you are envisioning a full-body secondary curve. The primary and secondary curves of your spine work together, much like shock absorbers, to lessen the impact from jumps.

The **cervical spine** consists of the top 7 vertebrae. This section of your spine has a slight natural secondary curve. Generally, your ears align over the center of your shoulders without tension.

The **thoracic spine** comprises the next 12 vertebrae below the cervical spine. The thoracic spine has a primary curve. Dancers sometimes stand up too straight in their attempts to have good posture, flattening the natural primary curve of the thoracic spine. This condition leads to excess tension in the upper back and neck. In this case, what looks like good posture is actually inefficient use of the upper back and neck muscles because they are engaged the whole time to hold the thoracic spine from its natural curve.

The **lumbar spine** comprises the 5 vertebrae below the thoracic vertebrae. The lumbar region is the most flexible section of the spine. The natural secondary curve in the lumbar spine is often enhanced. If you imagine a gymnast at the end of a routine with the lower back in an extreme curve, you are envisioning a condition called lumbar hyperlordosis. **Hyperlordosis** is an exaggeration of a secondary curve of the spine. Dancers often call this swayback (see figure 5.3).

Figure 5.3   Correct position of lumbar spine *(a)* and hyperlordosis *(b)*.

A properly aligned spine with its natural curves helps you move freely, efficiently, and without injury. Generally, from a side view, the ears should align over the shoulders, which align over the hips, which align over the knees and ankles.

Achieving proper alignment while standing still is one thing; keeping it while moving is vastly more difficult. Because proper alignment protects the joints and muscles of the body, the importance of returning to principles of proper alignment throughout jazz dance class is vital. Keeping your ankles from supinating or pronating, positioning your knees over the toes to avoid hyperextension, and using the natural curves of the spine are a foundation that underlies all of the following foot, arm, hand, and body positions.

ACTIVITY

BODY ALIGNMENT

Find a partner and take turns evaluating each other's body alignment from the side. First, partner A stands up naturally and lets partner B look at how your ankles, knees, hips, spine, and shoulders line up. Partner B notes whether some parts are more forward or more backward than others. Share this information with each other and then trade places, letting partner A observe partner B from the side. Write down the observations your partner made about your alignment and how you think this might affect your movement and dancing.

POSITIONS OF THE FEET

Jazz dance class uses both parallel foot positions and turned-out foot positions. In parallel foot positions, the feet may be side by side, apart at the distance of the center of the hip sockets, or in a wide position. Derived from classical ballet, the turned-out positions are called classical positions in jazz dance class.

Neutral position: feet apart at the distance of the center of the hip sockets and parallel to each other (see figure 5.4).

Figure 5.4   Neutral foot position.

First position: insides of the feet together and parallel to each other (figure 5.5).

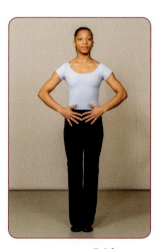

Figure 5.5   Parallel first position.

Second position: feet farther than hip-distance apart and parallel to each other (figure 5.6).

Figure 5.6 Parallel second position.

Fourth position: one foot forward of the other and the back heel lifted off the floor, as shown in figure 5.7 in plié.

Figure 5.7 Parallel fourth position.

Classical first position: feet in a V formation because of the natural turnout from the hip socket (figure 5.8).

Figure 5.8 Classical first position.

Figure 5.9 Classical second position.

Classical second position: feet apart about the length of one foot and naturally turned out (figure 5.9).

POSITIONS OF THE ARMS

As with the foot positions, jazz dance uses both its own arm positions as well as those commonly found in ballet. Positions of the arms in jazz dance vary from teacher to teacher and style to style. The list compiled in this book is extensive, but you may find your teacher using arm positions that are particular to that teacher or style of jazz. The teacher may even use the arm positions that appear here but with different names. The positions are broken down into three categories: jazz, classical, and additional. The jazz and classical arm positions parallel each other. The difference between the two is that the jazz arms are straight and angular, whereas the classical positions are rounded.

Jazz Arm Positions

These six jazz arm positions parallel the standard ballet arm positions, only with straight and angular shaping. Although the numbering of the arm positions varies from teacher to teacher, these jazz arm positions follow the most commonly found numbering system.

Preparatory position: arms bent in a 90-degree angle at the elbow, the hands in front of the hips, and the elbows out to the side (figure 5.10).

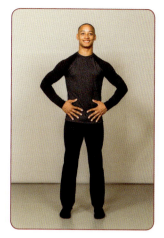

Figure 5.10 Preparatory position jazz arms.

First position: arms bent sharply at the elbows, hands in front of the chest, the middle fingers an inch (2.5 cm) apart, and elbows directly to the side (figure 5.11).

Figure 5.11 First-position jazz arms.

Second position: arms open from first position to the side and elbows slightly in front of the shoulder and slightly lower (figure 5.12).

Figure 5.12 Second-position jazz arms.

Third position: one arm in second position and the other arm in fifth position (raised above the head in line with the shoulder; figure 5.13).

Figure 5.13 Third-position jazz arms.

Fourth position: one arm in first position and the other arm in fifth position (figure 5.14).

Figure 5.14 Fourth-position jazz arms.

Fifth position: arms in a parallel position overhead and palms facing forward (figure 5.15).

Figure 5.15 Fifth-position jazz arms.

Classical Arm Positions

The classical arm positions in jazz dance derive from the ballet tradition. These rounded versions of the arm positions create a softer, flowing energy in contrast to the stronger, sharper energy of the jazz arm positions. Jazz dance makes use of both the stronger and softer arm positions.

Classical preparatory position: arms rounded and held in front of the body and tips of the middle fingers slightly apart and just below the navel (figure 5.16).

Figure 5.16 Preparatory position classical arms.

Classical first position: arms rounded and held in front of the body and tips of the middle fingers slightly apart and in front of the lower end of the sternum (figure 5.17).

Figure 5.17 First-position classical arms.

TECHNIQUE TIP

In these arm positions make sure that the upper part of your arm remains lifted and the tip of the elbow points directly back. If the tip of your elbow points downward, your upper arm will lose connection with your upper back, making the arms weak and ineffective.

Classical second position: arms rounded and held to the side of the body, elbows slightly in front of and lower than the shoulders, and wrists slightly in front of and lower than the elbows (figure 5.18).

Figure 5.18 Second-position classical arms.

Classical third position: arms rounded with one arm in classical second position and the other in classical fifth (raised above the head with the wrist in line with the shoulder; figure 5.19). Also commonly done with one arm in classical first instead of classical fifth position and called a middle third position.

Figure 5.19 Third-position classical arms.

Classical fourth position: arms rounded with one arm in classical first position and the other in classical fifth (raised above the head with the wrist in line with the shoulder; figure 5.20).

Figure 5.20 Fourth-position classical arms.

Classical fifth position: arms rounded and held overhead but slightly in front of the centerline of the body (figure 5.21).

Figure 5.21   Fifth-position classical arms.

Additional Arm Positions

Besides the jazz arm positions and the classical arm positions that parallel each other, a number of additional arm positions commonly apply to jazz dance. These arm positions come from a variety of jazz dance styles and may vary stylistically from teacher to teacher.

Sixth position: elbows moved from first position and lower in front of the body and the hands remain in front of the chest. The forearms are parallel (figure 5.22).

Figure 5.22   Sixth-position jazz arms.

Jack Cole position: Arms rounded and behind the body, elbows back, and forearms and hands below at hip level (figure 5.23). These arms, originally used by Jack Cole (considered the first person to teach a jazz dance class), have many names in the jazz dance tradition.

Figure 5.23 Jack Cole position arms.

Traditional jazz dance arm position: arms to the side and elbows bent so that the forearms are parallel to the floor. Hands are often in jazz hand position with palms facing front or, as in tap dance, natural hands with palms facing down (figure 5.24).

Figure 5.24 Traditional position jazz arms.

V position: arms held straight and above in the shape of the letter V (figure 5.25).

Figure 5.25 V arm position.

Middle parallel position: arms extended straight in front at shoulder height (figure 5.26). This position derives from jazz dance classes based on the Horton modern technique.

Figure 5.26 Middle parallel arm position.

Scoop position: arms rounded as in classical second but open to the ceiling rather than front and lifted high (figure 5.27).

Figure 5.27 Scoop arm position.

S-curve position: arms rounded as in classical second but with one open to the ceiling and the other open to the floor. Both arms are held to the side (figure 5.28).

Figure 5.28 S-curve arm position.

HAND POSITIONS

Jazz dance uses a variety of basic hand positions. In addition, the teacher or choreographer may use some personal stylistic favorites or make up completely new ones depending on the combination or phrase you are learning. Having a strong understanding of the basic hand positions will give you a foundation from which to begin.

Jazz hand position: fingers spread wide apart, palm slightly cupped, and fingers projecting out and forward (figure 5.29).

Figure 5.29 Jazz hand position.

Fist position: fingers curled in with the hand balled up in a fist (figure 5.30).

Figure 5.30 Fist hand position.

Natural position: hands held as if in a handshake, similar to the hand position in ballet but without the stylized separation of the fingers (figure 5.31).

Figure 5.31 Natural hand position, palm down *(a)* and natural hand position, palm up *(b)*.

Flex position: hand flexed at the wrist with the back of the hand close to 90 degrees from the arm (figure 5.32).

Figure 5.32 Flex hand position.

Classical position: hands held as in ballet, similar to the natural hand position but with the index finger lifted and the middle finger slightly lowered (for women; figure 5.33*a*). For men, the index finger lifts but the middle finger remains natural (figure 5.33*b*).

Figure 5.33 Classical hand position for women *(a)* and men *(b)*.

Bent position: a stylized hand with the wrist bent and the palm toward the arm at about 45 degrees (figure 5.34).

Figure 5.34 Bent hand position.

POSITIONS OF THE BODY

Body positions in jazz dance consist of standing, lunging, kneeling, seated, and floor positions. The basic body positions appear not only in exercises but also in combination and choreography. The rules of correct alignment apply in all the positions, so make sure to stay aware of them.

Flat back position: standing position with feet in neutral while bent at the hip sockets at 90 degrees so that the spine is elongated and parallel to the floor (figure 5.35).

Figure 5.35 Flat back position.

TECHNIQUE TIP

Avoid making the back literally flat. The natural curves of the spine should be maintained. When lowering into a flat back position, engage your abdominal muscles. When coming up to standing out of a flat back position, engage the muscles in the backs of your thighs and buttocks.

Lateral position: standing position with feet in classical second and the torso inclined toward one side. Both sides of the torso stay elongated and parallel to each other (figure 5.36).

Figure 5.36 Lateral position.

Forward lunge position: standing position with one foot forward and the knee bent at a 90-degree angle. The shin remains perpendicular to the floor. The back leg remains straight (figure 5.37).

Figure 5.37 Forward lunge position.

TECHNIQUE TIP

In the forward lunge position, keep the knee either directly above the ankle or let the front of your knee line up over the toes. Do not allow your knee to go beyond the toes because doing so can be dangerous to the knee joint.

Side lunge position: lunging to the side with one leg bent and the other straight and turned out to the side (figure 5.38).

Figure 5.38 Side lunge position.

Hinge position: aligned from the hips to the crown of the head and tilted backward in a second position parallel with knees bent (figure 5.39).

Figure 5.39 Hinge position.

Standing contraction position: a contraction of the whole spine performed in fourth position with knees bent (figure 5.40).

> ### TECHNIQUE TIP
>
> In the standing contraction, keep the entire spine curved and the shoulders aligned above the hips. If you take the shoulders farther forward than the hips, you begin to bend forward at the waist and lose the contraction.

Figure 5.40 Standing contraction position.

Butterfly position: seated position with the soles of the feet touching and the knees out to the side, the heels pulled toward the body, and the hands grasping the ankles (figure 5.41).

Figure 5.41 Butterfly position.

Seated first position: seated position with the legs extended to the front (figure 5.42).

Figure 5.42 Seated first position.

Seated second position: seated position with the legs extended to the side (figure 5.43).

Figure 5.43 Seated second position.

Cobra position: in a position lying on the front of the body, the hands are placed on the floor beneath the shoulders. The arms extend, taking the spine into an arch position (figure 5.44). This position derives from yoga.

Figure 5.44 Cobra position.

Scorpion position: cobra position with the knees bent. The toes reach toward the back of the head (figure 5.45). This position derives from yoga.

Figure 5.45 Scorpion position.

Bow position: in a position lying on the front of the body, the hands reach back to grasp the outside of the feet. The entire body is arched (figure 5.46). This position derives from yoga.

Figure 5.46 Bow position.

Cat position: knees on the floor directly below the hips and palms on the floor directly below the shoulders. Shins and feet rest on the floor. A full contraction of the spine from the crown of the head to the tip of the tailbone raises the middle of the back toward the ceiling (figure 5.47). This position derives from yoga.

Figure 5.47 Cat position.

Cow position: knees on the floor directly below the hips and palms on the floor directly below the shoulders. Shins and feet rest on the floor. A full arch of the spine from the crown of the head to the tip of the tailbone drops the abdomen toward the floor (figure 5.48). This position derives from yoga.

Figure 5.48   Cow position.

Triangle position: standing position with one foot forward and one foot behind, bent forward at the hip sockets over the front leg. Both legs are straight (figure 5.49).

Pretzel position: seated position with the legs bent, one leg lying on the floor, the foot of the other leg placed past the knee of the lower leg, the knee of the top leg pointing up, and the opposite arm wrapped around the top knee.

Figure 5.49   Triangle position.

These basic positions come into play in the exercises in the next chapters. Familiarity with their names and details will help you learn quickly. When the teacher calls for you to start in second position of the feet with Jack Cole position of the arms, you do not have to look for all the details of the shape if you already know these terms. Now, all you need to know is where in the room to begin when the teacher says to start upstage left.

STUDIO AND STAGE DIRECTIONS

Several approaches are used to give directions in the studio. Some systems number the walls and corners. When you get on a stage, however, specific terminology is used. Using stage terminology in the studio avoids the confusion from the various systems and prepares students who may go on to perform.

The stage directions come from the perspective that you are standing on the stage looking out at the audience (see figure 5.50). In the studio, this translates to your standing in class looking at the mirror. **Stage right**, from the viewpoint of the dancer onstage facing the audience or in the studio facing the front, is to

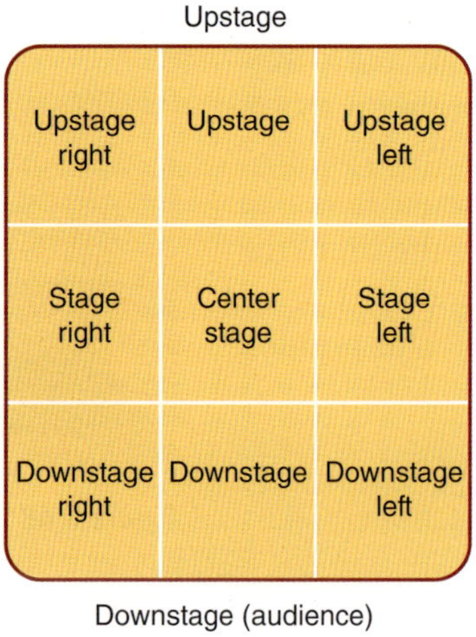

Upstage

Upstage right	Upstage	Upstage left
Stage right	Center stage	Stage left
Downstage right	Downstage	Downstage left

Downstage (audience)

Figure 5.50   Stage directions.

the dancer's right. **Stage left**, from the viewpoint of the dancer onstage facing the audience or in the studio facing the front, is to the dancer's left.

Center stage means the center of the stage or studio. **Upstage** is toward the back of the stage or studio. **Downstage** is toward the audience or front of the studio. Imagine if you were to put an orange upstage, it would roll downstage and into the audience.

By combining the right and left directions with the up and down directions, the studio space is covered. Given the direction to stand upstage left, if you face the mirror, you move to the left back corner of the studio.

These basic stage directions help orient you in the studio or on the stage. When the teacher instructs you to do a step center stage, you know where to do it. If the teacher instructs you to start stage left, you know which way to go. In addition, if the teacher tells you to do a combination from upstage left to downstage right, you know you will move along a diagonal pathway.

SUMMARY

With proper alignment, a vocabulary of positions, and an understanding of studio directions, you are ready to begin class. Remember to keep the jazz dance basics in mind as you get moving, referring back to them often. Proper alignment will help you move efficiently and safely, the basic positions will help you know what shapes to make with your body, and the stage directions will help you know where to go. Now you are ready to move.

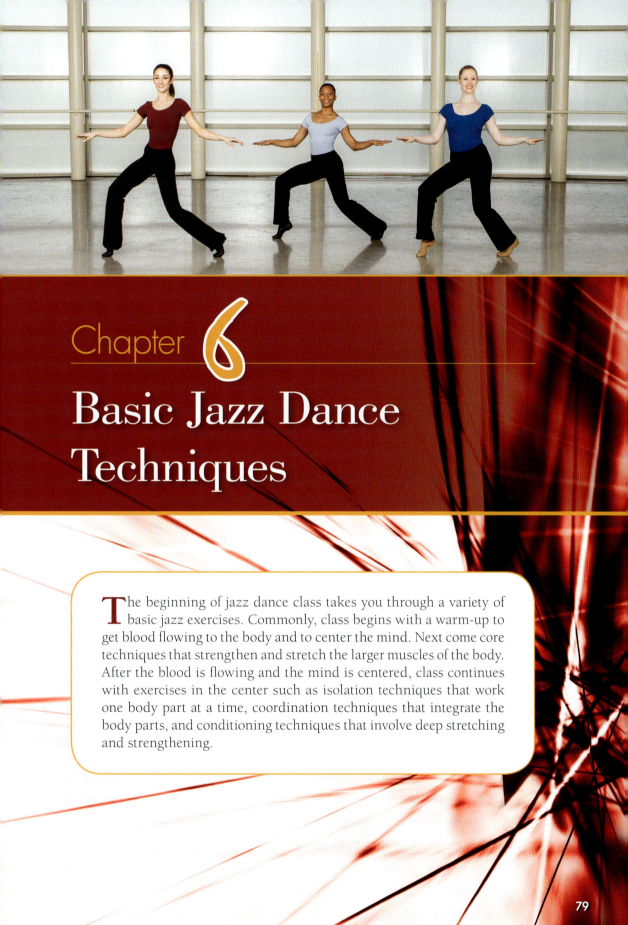

Chapter 6

Basic Jazz Dance Techniques

The beginning of jazz dance class takes you through a variety of basic jazz exercises. Commonly, class begins with a warm-up to get blood flowing to the body and to center the mind. Next come core techniques that strengthen and stretch the larger muscles of the body. After the blood is flowing and the mind is centered, class continues with exercises in the center such as isolation techniques that work one body part at a time, coordination techniques that integrate the body parts, and conditioning techniques that involve deep stretching and strengthening.

GETTING STARTED

In jazz dance class, the warm-up awakens the body by getting blood flowing to all the major muscle groups of the torso, legs, and arms. Jazz dance teachers tend to have their own signature warm-up. These warm-ups, however varied and unique, all serve the same purpose: to prepare the three bodies—the causal body, the subtle body, and the gross body—for the rest of jazz dance class.

The **causal body** is the part of our being that is aware of the present moment by being centered, focused, and mindful. The ritualistic repetition of the warm-up exercise and the consistency of it from class to class allows students to focus on the present moment and center themselves for the class ahead. Awareness of the causal body results in greater presence in the class and performance.

The **subtle body** is the part of our being that senses our inner energy fluctuations and neuromuscular connectivity. The subtle body's heightened understanding of the mind–body relationship—how you sense the space around you, how you sense your body, and how you sense your own movement patterns—lends itself to greater connection and coordination. Subtle-body sensitivity results in greater inner connectivity, expressiveness, and phrasing in movement.

The **gross body** is the part of our being made up of our physical muscles and bones. Gross-body conditioning results in increased strength, flexibility, endurance, and technical skill. A thorough gross-body warm-up helps prevent injuries by raising your body's core temperature and getting blood to flow to all your muscles. A comprehensive warm-up engages all three bodies so that they are primed for the rest of the class.

As you work on the warm-up techniques in this chapter, notice how engaging the three bodies enhances the experience and your ability to learn and enjoy jazz dance.

BASIC WARM-UP TECHNIQUES

Basic warm-up techniques consist of gross body-bending exercises to prepare your thigh muscles, rises up off your heels to prepare your ankles, and torso exercises to prepare your back and abdominals. The subtle body is prepared as your awareness of the energy awakens during the warm-up sequence. As you begin moving, you will sense where in your body you feel energized and where you feel tense or lethargic. Bringing attention to these subtle energies helps you approach the upcoming techniques intelligently—pushing for greater movement where there is energetic potential and easing into movement where there is energetic resistance. The causal body is prepared from the ritual of the warm-up, allowing you to center your mind by grounding you in the present moment of your physical being.

Demi Plié

Demi plié: half bent. A movement in which the knees bend while tracking directly over the toes. The heels remain on the floor.

Self-Check

- As in all exercises, focus on correct posture and correct placement of the toes over your knees in the demi pliés.
- When the tempo increases, keep the energy and placement consistent.

Grand Plié

Grande plié: big or large bend. A movement in which the knees bend deeply while tracking directly over the toes. The heels come off the floor in all foot positions except second and classical second.

Self-Check

- In the grand plié, the spine stays long. Avoid arching in your lower back.
- At the bottom of the demi plié, the heels come off the floor in all foot positions except second and classical second position.

> ### DID YOU KNOW?
>
> Although jazz dance grew for decades on its own, in the 1940s and '50s ballet-trained dancers and jazz dance cross-fertilized. Many of the French words from ballet were integrated into jazz dance. Because of this integration, jazz dancers use words like demi plié, grand plié, and relevé.

Relevé

Relevé: raised. A movement in which the heels raise off the floor with the weight balanced over the arches.

Self-Check

- Watch the alignment of your ankles; avoid rolling out over the pinky toe side of the feet.
- Rise up to a three-quarter position on the toes.
- Make sure that all toes remain on the floor and that weight is centered primarily over the heads of the metatarsals of the first two toes.
- Maintain proper alignment of the entire body throughout the relevé.

Flat Back

Flat back: a bend forward from the waist with the back and head in a long line.

> **TECHNIQUE TIP**
>
> Engage your hamstrings to initiate the rise from the flat back position.

Self-Check

- Keep your thoracic spine (upper back) from flattening. There should be a natural curve forward. Do not flatten the upper back in the attempt to achieve a straight spine.
- Initiate the lowering of the torso into the flat back position with a small contraction of your abdominal muscles.
- Engage your hamstrings to initiate the rise from the flat back position.
- Keep your weight primarily forward over the arches of your feet. Prevent locking in the back of the knees, especially if you have hyperextended knees.

Hinge

Hinge: aligned from the hips to the crown of the head and tilted backward with the feet in parallel position and the knees bent.

Self-Check

- Avoid the tendency to sit back in the hinge by dropping your pelvis. Keep the hips forward and in line with the crown of the head and heels.
- Engage your abdominal and thigh muscles to support yourself during the hinge.
- Maintain a long line from your knee to your hip and from your hip to your shoulder.

Horizontal Swing

Horizontal swing: swing of the torso from side to side in a flat back position.

Self-Check

- In the flat back left and flat back right, keep both sides of the torso equally long.
- Keep the head and neck in line with the spine at all times. Be careful not to look up while in the flat back position.
- Keep the weight over the arches of your feet. Prevent the knees from locking, especially in hyperextension.

Lateral

Lateral: a bend of the torso to the side while maintaining both sides of the torso parallel.

Self-Check

- Keep both sides of the torso equally long. Avoid curving the underside by maintaining equal distance from the hip to the armpit on both sides.
- Release into the hip opposite of the direction of the lateral to create a greater range of motion in the lateral.

The pliés, relevés, flat backs, hinges, horizontal swings, and laterals of the warm-up develop, stretch, and strengthen the legs and muscles supporting the trunk, back, abdominals, shoulders, hips, and ribs. These techniques make for a strong and expressive torso as well as help with elements that come later in class such as height in aerial movements, support in floor work and inversions, and control in turns.

BASIC ISOLATION TECHNIQUES

Basic isolation techniques work to mobilize one body part at a time to develop refined, specific control. Besides working each body part in isolation, isolation techniques may be combined to reconnect the different parts of the body, creating a layered combination that develops overall coordination and complexity in movement. Some body parts that can be worked in isolation include the head, shoulders, arms, hands, ribs, hips, legs, and feet.

Head Isolations

Sagittal head isolation: movement of the neck that creates the motion of the head looking up and down in the sagittal plane, as in nodding, "Yes."

Transverse head isolation: movement of the neck that creates the motion of the head looking side to side in the transverse plane, as in saying, "No."

Vertical head isolation: movement of the neck that creates the motion of the ear moving down toward either of the shoulders in the vertical plane, as in the movement of windshield wipers.

Head swing: movement of the neck and head from the tilt position on one side to the tilt position on the opposite side by passing the chin forward and down near the chest.

Head roll: movement of the neck and head in a complete circle, passing through all tilt and up and down positions.

Self-Check

- When looking up, keep the neck long by keeping the face parallel to the ceiling. Avoid going backward with the head and crunching the vertebrae of the neck.

- Keep your movements sharp and crisp by being specific with the positions.

> **SAFETY TIP**
>
> In the sagittal head isolation when the face goes up toward the ceiling, keep the neck long to avoid crunching the cervical vertebrae together by thinking that your cheekbones are going up to the sky. Crunching the neck bones creates stress on the fragile vertebrae of the neck. Use the same guideline during head rolls.

Sundari Head Isolations

Sundari head isolations: Head isolations in which the head remains upright and the center of the forehead is directly over the chin, moving side to side, front to back, or in a circular motion. Derived from Indian classical dance.

Shoulder Isolations

Shoulder shrug: lifting of one or both shoulders up toward the lower tips of the ears.

Shoulder roll: circular motion of one or both shoulders in the sagittal plane—forward, up, back, and down or the reverse.

Shoulder press: movement of one or both shoulders forward or back of the centerline of the body.

Self-Check

• Find your full range of motion in the shoulders by exaggerating each position.

• Avoid monotonous rhythms in shoulder movements by experimenting with impact and impulse phrase types discussed in chapter 1.

Arm Isolations

Basic jazz arm isolation: sequence of arm positions that goes (1) first, (2) sixth, (3) fifth, and (4) second. Can be reversed.

Stagger jazz arm isolation: sequence of arm positions based on the basic jazz arm isolation with one arm a count ahead of the other.

Arm isolations with hands: basic or stagger jazz arm isolations with hand isolations such as arms in first with flat hands, arms in sixth with fists, arms in fifth with jazz hands, and arms in second with flex hands.

Self-Check

• Keep the arm movements sharp and full of energy. A strong use of weight in the arms creates energy, whereas a light use of weight in the arms looks halfhearted.

• After you feel comfortable with the sequence of these exercises, explore the use of oppositional accents discussed in chapter 1.

Rib Isolations

Vertical rib isolation: movement of the spine that creates the image of the ribs moving side to side within the vertical plane.

Sagittal rib isolation: movement of the spine that creates the image of the ribs moving forward and back within the sagittal plane.

Diagonal rib isolation: movement of the spine that creates the image of the ribs moving both forward and side or back and side.

Circle rib isolation: movement of the spine that creates the image of the ribs circling, moving through the positions forward, side, back, and to the other side. Can be done in either direction.

Self-Check

- Make sure that you find your full range of motion by going to the edge of your movement capability in each position.
- Watch that your hips remain still during the rib isolations.

Hip Isolations

Straight hip isolation: movement of the hips directly side to side in the vertical plane.

Rock hip isolation: movement of the hips side to side while shifting weight onto the foot of the same side as the hip.

Swing hip isolation: movement of the hips side to side that drops into a deeper demi plié in the middle than at the sides. The hips trace the pathway of a smile.

Latin hip isolation: movement of the hips involving stepping on to one foot while pushing the opposite hip toward the opposite direction. Weight remains on the foot you have stepped on. Reverse directions.

Figure eight hips: movement of the hips making a circle to one side, passing through the center, and then circling to the other side. Can be done in either direction.

Hip circle: movement of the hips in a circle, moving through the positions forward, side, back, and to the other side. Can be done in either direction.

Self-Check

- In the swing hip, make sure to release into gravity on the drop in the center. Without the release, the sense of swing does not come through and the isolation looks contrived or forced.
- Notice the difference between the rock hip and Latin hip isolations. On the rock hip isolation, the hip goes toward the weight-bearing foot; on the Latin hip isolation, the hip goes away from the weight-bearing foot.

Leg Isolations

Forced arch: a weight-bearing position of the knee bent while simultaneously raised onto the ball of the foot on either one or both legs.

Double forced-arch leg isolation: sequence of legs that begins in classical first position of the feet and goes (1) knees bend, (2) forced arch, (3) straight knees on the ball of the foot, and (4) lower heels to classical first.

Single forced-arch leg isolation: sequence of legs that begins in classical second position of the feet and, with one leg only, goes (1) forced arch, (2) turn hip in, (3) turn hip out, and (4) return to classical second position.

Self-Check

- In forced arch, practice proper ankle alignment with the knees tracking over the first two toes without pressing into your knees.

- Keep the core engaged and strong throughout all isolations because the core is the source of power for a jazz dancer.

Now that you have worked each individual body part, try layering some of these techniques over one another. For example, try doing the single forced-arch leg isolation while simultaneously doing the basic jazz arm isolation. Better yet, try creating your own multilayered isolation exercise. The possibilities are countless. Bringing all the skills from isolation work back together is the focus of the coordination techniques you will look at next.

Jazz dancers use slow control when combining middle parallel arms and a side lunge descent. Exercises like this develop coordination and condition the body by building strength and flexibility.

BASIC COORDINATION TECHNIQUES

▶ With the individual body parts articulated from the isolation exercises, coordination techniques reintegrate the isolated body parts while developing correct posture, coordination of leg and arm movements, and articulation of the feet and ankles. Techniques from the warm-up may be included in the coordination exercises along with new techniques. These techniques, done standing in the center or at a ballet barre, come in many forms, from fast exercises to develop speed to slow exercises to develop control.

Tendu

Tendu: stretched. The working leg and foot stretch along the floor to a fully extended position. The foot is stretched, maintaining contact with the floor. Done starting from either first position or classical first position of the feet, tendu can be executed to the front, side, and back.

Self-Check

• The tendu to the side starting from classical first position of the feet is not directly to the side, but in the direction that the knee and toes are pointing when in classical first position of the feet and with outward rotation of the hip.

• Squeeze the inner thighs together to close the leg back into classical first position.

• Be careful not to lead with the heels when coming back into classical first position because doing so tends to cause the knee to bend on the way back in.

• Articulate (one at a time) the heel, ball, and toes of the foot on the way out to the stretched position. On the return, articulate the toes, ball, and heel.

Dégagé

Dégagé: to disengage. The working leg and foot stretch to full extension and then leave the floor at an angle of about 22 degrees.

Self-Check

• As in the tendu or stretch, squeeze the inner thighs together to close the leg back into classical first position.

• Articulate (one at a time) the heel, ball, and toes of the foot and then disengage from the floor on the way out to the stretched position. On the return, articulate the toes, ball, and heel.

> ### TECHNIQUE TIP
>
> On all moves that begin by sliding the foot and leg out to a stretched position, articulate (one at a time) the heel, ball, and toes of the foot on the way out to the stretched position. On the return, articulate the toes, ball, and heel.

En Croix

En croix: in the shape of a cross. This indicates that an exercise is to be executed in the following sequence of directions: to the front, to the side, to the back, and to the side.

Self-Check

- Make sure that the tendus (stretches) and dégagés (disengagements) to the side go in the direction of the knee and toes, not necessarily directly to the side of the body.
- Keep the hips as still as possible, isolating the leg in each of the directions in the en croix exercise.

Tendu Soutenu

Tendu soutenu: a stretch of the leg and foot to the fully extended position while the other leg bends simultaneously.

Self-Check

- In tendu soutenu, the stretching leg and the bending leg should begin and end at the same time. This technique requires control and attention to detail.
- Make sure that your weight is equally distributed on both feet when you return to the starting foot position.

Retiré

Retiré: withdrawn. A position with the foot alongside the knee of the other leg.

Self-Check

- Make sure that you are maintaining contact with the foot and the leg the entire way up to retiré and the entire way down.
- Imagine your big toe as the tip of a marker that draws a line up the leg and back down.

> ## DID YOU KNOW?
>
> A retiré (withdrawn) position is also frequently called passé. But passé, which means to pass through, is an action instead of a position. Although a passé can be done through the retiré position, passé can also be done through a number of other positions, such as when passing through first position or at the ankle.

Rond de Jambe

Rond de jambe: round of the leg, that is, a circular movement of the leg. Can be done on the ground or in the air and in either direction.

Self-Check

- When passing through the starting position of the feet, make sure that you completely return to the correct position even as you briefly move through it.
- In rond de jambe on the floor, think of drawing a large letter D with the big toe on the floor.

Grand Battement

Grand battement: big beat. A "kick" in which the working leg is raised as high as possible while the rest of the body stays still. Can be done to the front, side, or back. The technique is a controlled lift, not a throwing of the leg into the air, and the leg must be controlled while coming down.

Self-Check

- Brush the floor through a fully stretched leg and foot on the way to the grand battement.
- Keep the supporting leg and the spine straight.
- Avoid lifting one hip higher in the grand battement to the side.

Basic coordination techniques combine in a variety of ways to develop the coordination between the upper and lower body used in jazz dance. Jazz dancers need the ability to move the upper body both in complementary relationship to the lower body and in complete contrast. With the body fully warmed up by working individual body parts in isolations and the body reintegrated by performing coordination exercises, basic conditioning techniques focus on the development of increased flexibility and strength.

BASIC CONDITIONING TECHNIQUES

With the body warmed up and connected through isolation and coordination exercises, conditioning techniques work to develop the muscular system. Conditioning techniques may be done standing, kneeling, seated, or on the floor. They work to increase flexibility through dynamic stretching and develop strength through repetition. Although jazz dance techniques do develop some anaerobic endurance, their lack of aerobic activity—consisting of an elevated heart rate for 20 minutes or more—means that jazz dance conditioning does not develop consistent and proper aerobic endurance. Cross-training in aerobic activities, such as running and aerobic classes, is recommended to support aerobic development in jazz dance class.

Standing Contractions

Standing contraction: a contraction of the whole spine performed in fourth-position grand plié while moving the arms from classical second position into classical first position. Lengthen the legs and swipe the hand across the shoulders to return to the classical second position of the arms.

Self-Check

- Make sure that your shoulders remain directly above your hips. Avoid bending forward at the waist.
- Keep the weight evenly balanced between both feet in the grand plié.

Triangle Stretch

Triangle stretch: a stretch in a standing position with one foot forward and one foot behind, bent forward at the hip sockets over the front leg. Both legs are straight. This stretch can be done with both legs in parallel position or with the front leg parallel and the back leg naturally turned out.

Self-Check

• Try to keep your hips even and facing the front leg.
• Make a deep crease in the hip of the front leg as you bend forward to stretch.

Forward Lunge Stretch

Forward lunge stretch: a stretch from a standing position with one foot forward and the knee bent at a 90-degree angle. The shin remains perpendicular to the floor. The back leg remains straight, and the palms of both hands lie flat on the floor. For an increased stretch, place the forearm opposite the leg that is bent on the floor and reach the arm on the side of the bent leg to the ceiling. The spine spirals, and the head looks at the hand overhead. Then bring the overhead arm to place the forearm on the floor parallel with the other arm. Return to a forward lunge position with palms flat on the floor.

Self-Check

• Keep your knee directly over the arch of the foot and the shin perpendicular to the floor.
• Work to make your tailbone point down toward the floor.

Side Lunge Descent and Ascent

Side lunge descent and ascent: a stretch from the side lunge position with one leg bent and the other straight and turned out to the side. Lower until seated on the floor. To ascend, reach forward with the arms and return to the side lunge position.

Self-Check

• If necessary, lean your torso forward on the descent and ascent.
• Keep the foot and knee of the bent leg to the side so that you have room to descend and ascend.

Spiral Descent and Ascent

Spiral descent and ascent: a stretch beginning in forward lunge position. Turn the body toward the bent leg, allowing the other leg to bend, and come to a pretzel position seated on the floor. To ascend, reverse direction and return to the forward lunge position.

Self-Check

- Stay low to the floor and work for smooth control of the descent into the pretzel position and the ascent out of the pretzel position.
- For an added challenge, try the ascent and descent without using your hands for support.

Pretzel Stretch

Pretzel stretch: a stretch in a seated position with the legs bent, one leg lying on the floor, the foot of the other leg placed past the knee of the lower leg, the knee of the top leg pointed up, and the opposite arm wrapped around the top knee.

Self-Check

- Concentrate on a gentle spiral coming up from the tip of your tailbone all the way up your spine and out the top of your head.
- With the arm wrapped around the knee, pull gently to increase the stretch while looking over the opposite shoulder.

Heel Stretch

Heel stretch: a stretch in a seated position, extending one leg forward or to the side while holding on to the inside of the foot, heel, or ankle.

Self-Check

- Remain seated on the floor by avoiding the tendency to lift one buttock up off the ground while stretching.
- Lengthen the lumbar spine as you stretch.

Butterfly Stretch

Butterfly stretch: a stretch in a seated position with the soles of the feet touching and the knees open to the side, the heels pulled toward the body, and the hands grasping the ankles. The torso can move forward in flat back or rounded position.

Self-Check

- Make sure to grab your ankles, not your toes.
- When bent forward, imagine a deep crease in your hips.

Seated First-Position Stretch

Seated first-position stretch: a stretch with a full forward bend in a seated position with the legs extended to the front.

Self-Check

- Keep the backs of the knees long as you stretch forward.
- As you inhale, imagine your muscles filling up like a long balloon and lengthening. As you exhale, imagine all the air escaping and release deeper into the stretch.

Seated Second-Position Stretch

Seated second-position stretch: a stretch with a full forward bend or over each of the legs while in a seated position with the legs extended à la seconde.

Self-Check

- When stretching over one leg, keep the buttock of the opposite side on the floor.
- Turn your shoulders so that they squarely face the leg over which you stretch.

Cobra Stretch

Cobra stretch: a stretch performed while lying down on the front of the body with the hands placed on the floor beneath the shoulders and the arms extended to take the spine into an arched position.

Self-Check

- Keep the front of the hips in contact with the floor.
- Think of lengthening through the entire spine, imagining space between each vertebra.

Scorpion Stretch

Scorpion stretch: a stretch performed while lying down on the front of the body with the hands placed on the floor beneath the shoulders, the arms extended to take the spine into an arched position, the knees bent, and the toes reaching toward the back of the head.

Self-Check

- Remain long as you stretch in this position; avoid bending sharply in the lower back.
- Breathe deeply in this stretch to relieve unnecessary stress.

Bow Stretch

Bow stretch: a stretch performed while lying down on the front of the body with the hands reaching back to grasp the outside of the feet. The feet press against the hands, raising the body into a full body arch.

Self-Check

- Keep pressure away from the lower back by imagining the body arching in a long, spacious arc.
- Keep the thighs and knees parallel to each other.

> **SAFETY TIP**
>
> The cobra, scorpion, and bow stretches derive from yoga practice. Imagine a long line of energy through the spine to avoid compressing the vertebrae of the spine. Think of these positions as long, gentle lines of arcing energy rather than severe and static curves of the spine.

Cat and Cow Stretch

Cat and cow stretch: a stretch of the torso performed with the knees on the floor directly below the hips and the palms on the floor directly below the shoulders, alternating between cat position and cow position.

Self-Check

- When stretching in the cow position, look toward the ceiling.
- When stretching in the cat position, look toward your navel.

Leg Lifts

Leg lifts: a strengthening exercise (that also stretches) executed while lying on the back, supported on the forearms, by lifting one leg at a time directly forward in line with the shoulder.

Self-Check

- Keep the hip of the lifting leg down on the floor.
- Make sure that the leg remaining on the floor stays straight while the other leg lifts.

Split Stretch

Split stretch: a stretch of the legs with one leg directly forward of the body and the other leg directly back, lowering toward the ground and supported by the hands on either side of the leg.

Self-Check

- Go only as far as your body will allow, but keep both knees straight.
- Work at your own pace to find a productive stretch for your body. Pushing too hard can lead to injury, and not pushing enough wastes time. Find your personal edge and work there.

Push-Ups

Push-ups: a traditional strengthening exercise for the arms and upper body that may be done with knees touching the floor, with the legs straight on the balls of the feet, or with one leg lifted off the floor.

Self-Check

• Work to maintain a long line from the knees up through the top of the head.

• Engage your abdominal muscles.

Abdominal Curls

Abdominal curls: a traditional strengthening exercise for the abdominal and core muscles done from a position lying on the back, with knees bent, and lifting up so that the shoulder blades come up from the floor.

Self-Check

• Make sure that you avoid pushing your abdominal muscles out.

• Keep your neck long by avoiding pulling your head with your hands to come up from the floor.

Basic conditioning techniques improve your flexibility while also building muscular strength. Having a well-conditioned body not only helps you learn jazz dance skills and steps with greater ease but also helps prevent unnecessary injuries. Conditioning techniques are a vital part of your jazz dance class.

SUMMARY

After performing the basic jazz dance techniques in the warm-up, isolation, coordination, and conditioning exercises, your body should be warm, you should be perspiring, and you should be ready to move. The next chapter explores exercises done in the center and across the floor that begin to develop specific jazz dance skills, steps, and techniques.

To find supplementary materials for this chapter, such as learning activities, e-journal assignments, and web links, visit the web resource at **www.HumanKinetics.com/BeginningJazzDance.**

WEB RESOURCE

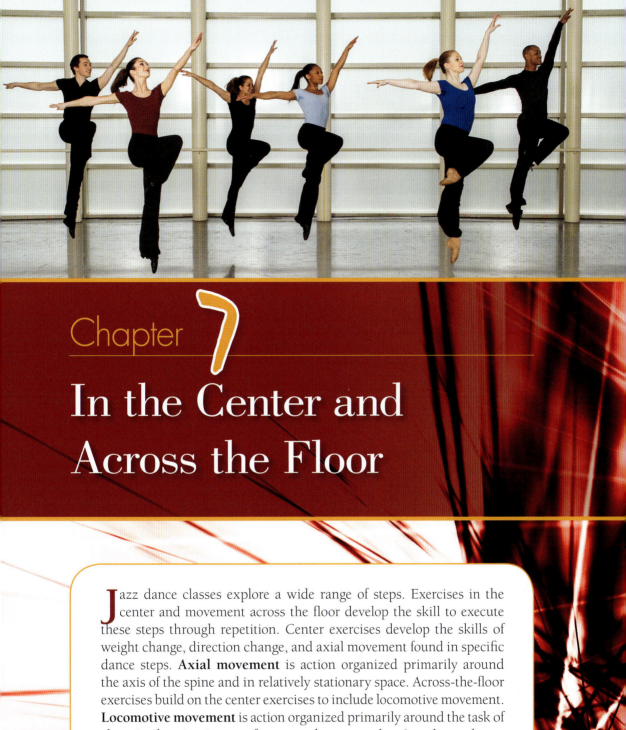

Chapter 7

In the Center and Across the Floor

Jazz dance classes explore a wide range of steps. Exercises in the center and movement across the floor develop the skill to execute these steps through repetition. Center exercises develop the skills of weight change, direction change, and axial movement found in specific dance steps. **Axial movement** is action organized primarily around the axis of the spine and in relatively stationary space. Across-the-floor exercises build on the center exercises to include locomotive movement. **Locomotive movement** is action organized primarily around the task of changing location in space from one place to another. Jazz dance classes commonly culminate in learning combinations or phrases that include all the previously developed skills and steps, both axial and locomotive. A cool-down sequence at the end allows the mind and body to refocus and signals the completion of the class.

EXERCISES IN THE CENTER

Exercises in the center include axial movement and popular dance steps from the simple to the complex. These exercises focus on

- quick changes of weight;
- sharp changes of direction;
- bending, extending, and rotating joint actions;
- spiraling of the spine;
- gestures of the limbs; or
- any combination of those.

Many of those steps derive from authentic and traditional jazz dance traditions, but they can be found in contemporary social dance steps with updated rhythms and stylistic changes. The following steps progress from basic patterns to complex patterns within each category.

Step and Step Variations

In jazz dance, step and step variations focus on the shifting of weight. This understanding of the shifting of weight forms the foundation for all jazz dance steps and techniques done in place and while traveling through space.

Step

Step: a transfer of weight from the ball, heel, or full foot of one foot to the ball, heel, or full foot of the other foot. Knowing when and when not to transfer weight is the foundation for many basic jazz dance steps. Pay attention to where your weight is while you learn techniques and steps.

Self-Check

- Make sure that you fully transfer your weight.
- Try all variations of the step—with weight on the heel, toe, and full foot—to get a sense of the shift of weight needed.
- Knowing when and when not to transfer weight is the foundation for basic jazz dance steps. Pay attention to where your weight is while you learn techniques and steps.

Touch

Touch: contacting the floor with a foot without transferring weight. A touch can be done with the ball, heel, or full foot, but it does not include a transfer of weight. In basic jazz dance steps, a touch with a foot usually indicates that the same foot will do the next action involving the feet.

Self-Check

- Notice whether you should be performing the touch with the ball, heel, or full foot.
- Do not transfer your weight.
- Notice that the touching foot remains free of weight and ready to do the next action involving the feet.

Step Touch

Step touch: a step with either foot with a transfer of weight followed by a touch with the opposite foot without the transfer of weight. Both the step and the touch can be done side to side, forward, or back and with the ball, heel, or full foot.

Self-Check

- Make sure that you perform the step touch to the beat of the music.
- Practice the step touch side to side, forward, and back.
- For variety, touch by crossing in front of the standing leg or by crossing behind the standing leg.

Step Together Step Touch

Step together step touch: a step to the side with the first foot, a step together with the second foot, a step to the side again with the first foot, and a touch with the second foot to finish.

Self-Check

- Practice the step together step touch side to side, forward, and backward.
- Relax your knees and feel the natural bounce while executing this step.
- Try clapping on the downbeat and then the upbeat to discover which one feels and sounds best.

Jazz Square

Jazz square (also called jazz box): four steps in the pattern of a square on the floor. Cross over front, step back, step side, and step front.

Self-Check

- Imagine a square painted on the floor and step on all four corners of that square.
- For variation, touch instead of step on the last step and repeat on the other side.
- For an added challenge, try simultaneously executing the basic arm isolation from chapter 6.

Ball Change

Ball change: a step behind but without traveling on the ball of one foot followed by a step in place of the other foot. Rhythmically, this step can be performed in duple meter, counted "and 1," or in triple meter, counted "a 1."

Self-Check

- Be patient with yourself. The weight shift in the ball change is an important coordination in beginning jazz dance that will influence many future steps.
- After you learn the ball change, challenge yourself to try the step in both duple meter and triple meter.

Pas de Bourrée

Pas de bourrée (also called cross ball change): a three-part step. Cross one foot in back (or in front) of the second foot, step the second foot to the side, and step the first foot in place or slightly in front. Rhythmically, this step is commonly performed in duple meter, counted "1 and 2."

> ### TECHNIQUE TIP
>
> When performing the pas de bourrée (or cross ball change), remember to stay low in plié the entire time. Traditionally, the jazz pas de bourrée is done this way with a low center of gravity to express power and to cover ground. Rising up and down during pas de bourrée loses the connection with gravity and, therefore, its power.

Self-Check

- The knees remain bent except for the step out to the side, which extends fully and bears weight on the ball of the foot.
- Be mindful of the tendency to accent the third step of the pas de bourrée (the change of the cross ball change). The second step (which falls on the upbeat) is the visually accented step (the ball of the cross ball change) and should be where the accent falls.

Kimbo

Kimbo: a step back on one foot while flexing and raising the toe of the other foot.

Self-Check

• Try this step both traveling back and staying in place.

• For a greater challenge, try this step in different rhythms: "1, 2, 3 and 4" or "5 and 6, 7 and 8."

Chug

Chug: a slide forward without leaving the ground on one or both feet, with knee or knees bent. Can also be done with the slide to the back.

Self-Check

• Each chug should end with knee or knees bent.

• The heel lifts off the floor to start the slide, but the ball of the foot remains in contact with the floor at all times.

• Stay with the music. The landing of the chug should be right on the beat.

Step Together Step

Step together step (also called side chassé): can be done to the side as a single step or with continuously alternating legs and directional facing.

Self-Check

• Emphasize covering ground side to side over going for height.

• After you have the basic coordination, make sure that with each step you contact the floor with the toes first, then the ball of the foot, and then the heel.

• Try changing sides with each step together step so that you do one facing the front and then turn halfway around to face the back before doing the next step together step facing back.

Basic step and step variations develop the ability to make the clear, articulate weight shifts that underlie all jazz dance steps. As you learn a new step or combination in jazz dance class, clarifying for yourself when weight is shifted and when it is not aids in learning the material. Jazz dancers excel at intricate and rhythmic weight shifts.

Hop, Jump, and Leap Steps and Variations

▶ Hop, jump, and leap steps include all steps that elevate the entire body off the floor and into the air. These steps are exciting to perform and watch. Adequate strength and proper use of the feet, ankles, and knees become extremely important in elevations because of the force of the weight of the body returning to the floor.

Hop

Hop: from one foot, going into the air and landing on the same foot. Hops can be small, medium, or large and performed in various positions of the feet, legs, and body.

> ### DID YOU KNOW?
>
> In dance, a hop goes from one foot to the same foot. The bunny hop, a popular social dance novelty, is really a jump because it involves both feet.

Self-Check

- In hops and in all elevations, begin and end with the knees bent to protect the health of your knees.
- Roll through the ball of the foot on the way up to create more height in the hop.
- Roll through the ball of the foot on the landing for a controlled descent.

Jump

Jump: any elevation going into the air that involves taking off or landing on two feet. Basic jumps take off from two feet and land on two feet. Jumps that are more complicated include those that take off from two feet and land on one foot and those that take off from one foot and land on two feet. Jumps can be small, medium, or large and can be performed starting in various positions, taking various positions in the air, and landing in various positions.

Self-Check

- Make sure to begin and land with your knees bent and tracking over your big toes.
- As your body descends into the knee bend in your landing, feel a counterpull up away from the floor to avoid rolling in or out at the ankles.

Jump Apart Together

Jump apart together: a jump apart from first position of the feet with arms in sixth position to second position of the feet with arms in V position followed by a jump back to the starting position.

Self-Check

• For variation, when jumping to second position of the feet, rise to the balls of the feet (relevé).

• For added challenge, stagger it by having the leg and arm of one side arrive a split second before the other side. This version of the step is also called a scarecrow.

Straight Jump

Straight jump: a jump from two feet straight up with the arms in fifth position.

Self-Check

• From the tips of the toes to the tips of the fingers, extend fully at the height of the jump.

• For variation, open the arms to second at the height of the jump.

Tuck Jump

Tuck jump: a jump while withdrawing both legs underneath the body with the arms in fifth position.

Self-Check

• Lift the knees high to the front and bring the heels up underneath your buttocks.

• For variation, open the arms to second at the height of the jump.

Arch Jump

Arch jump (also called a C jump): a jump from two feet straight up, arching the back at the height of the jump, and at the same time reaching the legs to the back and the arms overhead. Can also be done to the side.

> ### SAFETY TIP
> When performing an arch jump, think of the spine as a long, gentle curve that reaches out the top of the head and out the legs. Avoid sharply arching the back so that you do not compress the vertebrae of the spine.

Self-Check

• Keep the energy in the arch extending through all the limbs. The spine creates the shape explored in the scorpion during warm-up.

• For variation, circle the arms up and to the back at the height of the jump and then down to cross in front in the landing.

• Try the arch to the side, taking both legs in the direction of the arch.

Pike Jump

Pike jump: a jump from two feet into a pike (seated first) position, bent at waist, legs straight and together, and arms reaching down at the sides.

Self-Check

• This jump is a good strengthening exercise because performing it requires height and strong abdominals.

• For variation, open the arms to second at the height of the jump.

Assemblé

Assemblé: assembled. A jump that takes off from one foot and lands on two feet. Bend your knees, lift one leg, and jump into the air. Bring both legs together ("assemble" them) while in midair and land on both feet with the knees bent. Can be done in any direction.

Self-Check

• Try this variation by beginning on both feet. Brush one leg and foot through the fully extended position, disengaging from the floor and then jumping into the air.

• Assemble the legs in the air before landing with bent knees.

Sissonne

Sissonne: a jump from both feet onto one foot. Can be done front, side, and back.

Self-Check

• Bend your knees and jump equally off both feet.

• When in the air, point both feet fully.

• Land on one leg with the leg bent and the other leg remaining in the air.

Leap

Leap: from one foot, going fully into the air in any direction and in any position before landing on the opposite foot. Leaps can be small, medium, or large and done in place or by traveling through space. They can also be done starting, moving through, and ending in a variety of feet, leg, and body positions.

Self-Check

• All the suggestions for hops and jumps also apply to leaps, such as using bent knees, rolling through the feet, keeping the knees over the toes, and avoiding rolling in or out at the ankles.

• The most common large leap in jazz dance is the grand jeté, a forward leap in which both legs strive to stretch out parallel to the floor, one in front and one in back, during the moment in the air.

Hop, jump, and leap steps add dynamic and energetic accents to jazz dance. They are not only interesting to watch but also thrilling to perform. Taking flight in a powerful, expressive jazz dance hop, jump, or leap brings an exhilarating feeling to class.

Traditional Jazz Steps

Traditional jazz steps derive from historical jazz dance styles. These steps include weight shifts and elevations combined with characteristic body positions and arm gestures. In this section, they are presented in historical order, starting with the oldest. Often, traditional jazz steps are recycled into new dance styles. As you explore these steps, see whether you can recognize aspects or even the whole step in current dance styles.

Flick Kick

Flick kick: a kick performed by lifting a knee while bent, extending the leg sharply, and then bending it again on the way down. This step can be done small, medium, or large.

Self-Check

- The extension should be sharp, like a flicking motion.
- Keep the supporting leg and the spine straight.

Cakewalk

Cakewalk: a leaping kick forward that begins with a small leap onto one foot while the other leg flick kicks and is then immediately repeated on the other side. This step is often done with the torso leaning slightly backward.

> **DID YOU KNOW?**
>
> The cakewalk was a popular dance tradition among slaves on plantations in the 19th century. White performers appropriated the step and presented it in minstrel shows.

Self-Check

- The extension should be sharp, like a flicking motion.
- Keep the supporting leg and the spine straight.
- Leap immediately after the flick kick onto that same leg to repeat on the other side.

Sugar

Sugar: starts with the feet in jazz second position and weight equally on both feet. Change weight to the ball of the left foot and pivot to the right on the ball of the left foot until the left toe is pointed to the right. At same time step on ball of the right foot with the toe pointed to the right. Reverse. The step can be done on a straight leg or with knees bent, on the balls of the feet, or on the whole foot.

Self-Check

- Let the hips switch from side to side but keep the torso facing front.
- Stay on the balls of the feet and stay with the music. Try changing tempos.

Charleston

Charleston: a step forward on one foot, small flick kick forward with the other foot, step back with the free foot, and then touch behind with the original foot.

Self-Check

- For variation, try the 1920s flapper version by replacing the flick kick with a touch forward, turning the feet in on the upbeat, and turning them out on each step and touch.
- To try the 1940s Lindy hop version of the Charleston, do a low flick kick forward with the left while making a small hop on the right. Make a small leap on the left while doing a low flick kick forward with the right and then hop on the left. Do a low flick kick to the side with the right foot, step back on the right foot, and finish with a ball change back front with the left foot and then the right foot. Repeat. Try reversing feet.

Shorty George

Shorty George: a step with the knees together, stepping slightly forward on one foot while swinging the knees and hips to the same side as the stepping foot with the heels barely off the ground. Repeat to the other side and in sequence.

Self-Check

- The Shorty George was named after jitterbug and Lindy hop dancer "Shorty" George Snowden in the 1930s. He could do this step underneath his partner's long legs.
- Make this step fun. Find your own way of doing it and don't try to be too correct.

Crazy Legs

Crazy legs: a step done with the knees bent and a forced arch on both feet. On the "and" count, both knees open up as weight shifts to one foot. On the "a" count, both knees return to the original position. The step was popularized in the 1940s in the Lindy hop.

Self-Check

- This step should create the comical effect of the legs looking as if they are made of rubber.
- Stay off the heels the entire time.

Scissor Step

Scissor step: a small leap onto one foot while extending the opposite leg to the side with the heel touching the floor and then doing a ball change underneath yourself, leading with the extended leg and repeating on the other side.

Self-Check

- The flexed foot is the one that does the ball of the ball change on the way back in.
- After the coordination and sequence of the feet are consistent, work on staying with the beat.

These jazz dance students are performing the scissor step, a quick footwork step that requires the coordination of a small leap, a touch, and a ball change.

Flea Hop

Flea hop: a step done with weight on one foot and the other foot raised with a flexed knee. Slide to the raised foot on the standing foot and step down with the raised foot. Reverse. Free leg position may be varied. Done as skipping side to side.

Self-Check

• Initiate the movement by pushing off the floor with the standing foot.
• For an added challenge, increase the size of the slide.

Lindy

Lindy: step together step followed by a ball change.

Self-Check

• This step was named in the 1940s after the aviator Charles Lindbergh, who was a celebrity when this step was a popular social dance.
• For an added challenge, extend the arms to second on the step together step and return to preparatory or cross in front on the ball change.
• For variation, replace the step together step with a step to the side and slide of the second foot before the ball change.

Truckin'

Truckin': a movement consisting of a step hop forward with the index finger wagging side to side.

Self-Check

• Say, "Step hop" to get the rhythm and weight change of this step.
• Try traveling forward, back, and in patterns with this step.

Pony

Pony: a 1960s social dance step of a small leap (or spring) to the side onto one foot followed by a step onto the other foot beside the starting foot and ending with a step in place of the original foot. Repeat on other side.

Self-Check

• Lift up the knees to create a bouncy and energetic quality.
• Try traveling forward, back, and in patterns with this step.

Traditional jazz steps allow room for personal flair and style. After you have the basic feel for these steps, find your own way of expressing them. Traditional jazz steps derive from historical social dance trends but have intricate weight-shift patterns that make them important for jazz dance students still today.

Turns

Basic jazz dance turns are steps in which the body turns around its axis or changes directional facing, sometimes accomplishing both at the same time. These basic turns include variations on turning around the axis while standing in place as well as traveling through space.

Mess Around

Mess around: a turning step in which one foot steps across in front of the other, twisting the legs, followed by an unwinding in the direction of the foot in front to complete a full revolution.

Self-Check

- Find a spot in front of you at the start and keep focused on it as long as possible.
- When you can no longer hold the spot, quickly turn the head to find it again, before finishing the turn with the body.

Pivot Turn

Pivot turn: a turning step that begins with a step forward on one foot and follows with a turn on the ball of the front foot to face a new direction. Can be done with quarter or half turns.

Self-Check

- Use a sharp and clean spot, looking over the shoulder before changing.
- For a challenge, add the basic arm isolation to a set of two pivot turns.

Three-Step Turn

Three-step turn: a step together step touch done while turning once toward the leg on which the first step is taken.

Self-Check

- Spot in the direction of the turn and then look front on the touch.
- For added challenge, for a turn to the right, start with right arm in classical first and the left arm in classical second. On the first step, open the arms to classical second. On the second step, close the arms to classical first. On the third step, open the arms to classical second. On the touch, close the left arm to classical first, leaving the right arm in classical second. Reverse for the turn to the left.

Paddle Turn

Paddle turn: a series of quick ball changes done while the body is rotating.

Self-Check

- Make spatial directions clean and clear.
- The paddle or rise onto the ball of the foot falls on the upbeat. The body rises up and down with the beat.
- For a challenge, try it double time or to faster music.

Pas de bourrée turn

Pas de bourrée turn (also called cross ball change turn): a three-part turn. The first foot crosses in back of the second foot while revolving toward the same shoulder as the foot crossing behind. Then the second foot steps to the side while completing the revolution. The first foot steps in place or slightly front. Rhythmically, this step is commonly performed in duple meter, counted "1 and 2." This can be done as a quarter, half, three-quarter, or full turn.

Self-Check

- The knees remain bent except for the step out to the side, which extends fully and bears weight on the ball of the foot.
- Use a strong spot to maintain clear directional facing.

Turning steps require the jazz dance student to have a strong sense of direction because the studio spins around momentarily. As you come out of a turn and go into a step or elevation, the change from one type of movement to another is visually interesting to the viewer and challenging for the dancer. The strong use of visual focus and spatial direction makes jazz dance students agile movers.

The use of quick changes of weight; sharp changes of direction; bending, extending, and rotating joint actions; spiraling of the spine; and gestures of the limbs in center exercises prepares you for work across the floor. Across-the-floor exercises include new steps and skills, but you may see the center exercises you have learned appear in traveling phrases across the floor in their stationary forms or be made to travel on their own.

EXERCISES ACROSS THE FLOOR

Exercises done across the floor incorporate the same elements as those done in the center, but they emphasize moving through space. In exercises across the floor, jazz walks, footwork, turns, elevations, and floor work are explored while traveling from one place to another in space.

Jazz Walks and Footwork

Jazz dance uses stylized walks and intricate footwork. A variety of walks and runs mix with weight and direction changes, making rhythmically challenging steps unique to the jazz dance class. The walks and footwork in this section are listed as progressions that increase in difficulty from one to the next.

Basic Jazz Walk

Basic jazz walk: walking forward with legs extending between steps and maintaining a low center of gravity with legs and feet turned out. Can also be done in parallel.

Self-Check

- First, focus on toe-ball-heel, perhaps saying it as you do it.

- Keep a low center of gravity the entire way across the floor. This low center of gravity gives jazz dance its powerful dynamic.

- Pick a focal point ahead of you in the distance to keep from looking down at the floor or your feet.

> **TECHNIQUE TIP**
>
> The use of a low center of gravity gives jazz dance its powerful quality and also allows the legs to take longer steps which travel through space more dynamically. Stay low in your jazz walks and you will travel more!

Jazz Chassé

Jazz chassé: a step together step to the front that can be done as a single step or with continuous alternating legs.

Self-Check

- The toes should make contact with the floor first on each step.

- Focus on keeping a low center of gravity, as in the jazz walk, the entire way across the floor.

- Notice that "chassé" is similar to "chase." The back leg "chases" the front leg away.

Grapevine

Grapevine: a step to the side followed by a step of the other leg crossing in front and then another step to the side followed by a step crossing back in a continuous sequence.

Self-Check

- Keep the beat of the music while performing this step at first.
- For a greater challenge, bend the knees on the crossing steps and straighten them on the side steps with your focus front the entire time.

Susie Q

Susie Q: a step in which one foot crosses in front of the other while at the same time both knees bend and turn toward the direction of the step. Next, the other foot steps in the same direction while the heel of the first foot stays on the floor with the toe pointing up.

Self-Check

- Allow the hips to swivel from side to side with the steps.
- For an added challenge, hold the arms in front of the body with the hands flexed. The arms move from side to side in opposition with the first foot (the one that goes toe up).

Triplet

Triplet: a step forward on one foot with the knee bent followed by two consecutive steps with the legs straight on the balls of the feet (down–up–up).

Self-Check

- Make the difference in levels (down and up) clear.
- The step with the knees bent should feel like a slight fall down and forward that creates the momentum for movement.

Jazz Run

Jazz run: long, reaching, darting run across the floor with a low center of gravity.

Self-Check

- Stay low to the ground. Imagine a low ceiling that you would hit your head on if you came up out of the depth of the knee bend during the run.
- Reach long with the front and back leg in the run but do not leap off the floor.

Camel Walk

Camel walk: a step forward in parallel onto one foot in forced-arch position while the other foot remains flat, on the ground, and weightless. Alternate. Can also be done sliding the foot. Both variations can be done in reverse.

Self-Check

- Be patient; this step does not cover a lot of ground.
- Try doing it in place and with different rhythms.

> **TECHNIQUE TIP**
>
> The trick to the camel walk is to make sure that the weight is on the foot in forced-arch position and not on the foot that remains flat on the floor. This creates an illusion that is used in many other steps like Cuban walks and the moonwalk (a backwards, sliding camel walk once known as the Bill Bailey).

Hitch Glide

Hitch glide: a short slide on the ball of the foot across the floor in any direction while the free leg is placed at the side of the knee (retiré).

Self-Check

- The energy for the hitch comes from the opposite leg coming quickly to the side of the knee.
- Swinging the arms in opposition helps get more force for glide in the hitch.

Cat Walk

Cat walk: walking like a cat by crossing one leg in front of the other and peeling the back heel off the floor into a forced-arch position.

Self-Check

- Pick up the foot before touching it forward like a cat flicking litter behind it (the image isn't pretty, but it works).
- The back foot in forced arch should carry weight just before the transfer happens. If the weight transfers before the forced-arch position is reached, the movement looks like a regular jazz walk.
- Imagine a cat walking on a narrow tree limb.

Triple Step

Triple step: a triplet-like step that is performed up-up-down, turning toward the leg on the third step and dragging the opposite foot.

Self-Check

- The arms are free flowing and do not hit specific positions. Instead, focus on floating up on the upbeat and the following "and" and coming down sharply (a whipping or slashing action) all on the downbeat.
- Compare this step to a triplet that goes down–up–up in three counts. The triple step goes up-up-down all in two counts, "1 and 2."
- Turn toward the foot that is stepping down.

Jazz Strut

Jazz strut: a jazz walk in which the leg lifts to a position with the foot aside the knee (retiré) of the standing leg before stepping forward.

Self-Check

- This version of the jazz walk combines the basic jazz walk with the accented leg and crossover of the cat walk, executed in syncopation and counted "a 1."
- Keep the head focused strongly forward.
- Keep the chest and head lifted.

Drag Step

Drag step: a darting step sideways with one knee bent while dragging the free foot across the floor.

Self-Check

- Leap (or spring) out slightly onto the first step to create an accent and energy.
- Push the leading hip out to the side to take the body off center for added excitement.

Vegas Walk

Vegas walk: A jazz strut with straight legs done on the balls of the feet or on flat feet.

Self-Check

- The version of the jazz strut done while on the balls of the feet is a common step for Vegas showgirls who are working in high heels.
- The male version of this step is commonly done on a flat foot.
- Try adding alternating shoulder rolls of the same side as the forward foot.

Moonwalk (Michael Jackson)

Moonwalk (Michael Jackson): A backward sliding camel walk. Michael Jackson popularized this step in 1984, but it is a variation of a vaudeville step called the Bill Bailey. Like most pop and hip-hop dancers, Jackson drew from the rich jazz dance tradition.

Self-Check

• The weight on the forced-arch foot creates an illusion of weightlessness that is found in a variety of traditional steps such as the camel walk, Cuban walk, and Bill Bailey and in break dance and hip-hop choreography.

Moonwalk (Bob Fosse)

Moonwalk (Bob Fosse): From the style of Bob Fosse, a step onto forced arch with the back leg turned out and bent, done in slow motion as if walking on the moon.

Self-Check

• This step, popularized by musical theater choreographer Bob Fosse, has a smooth weightless quality, as if walking on the moon.

• The torso pitches slightly forward with each step.

Stylized jazz walks and footwork continue to develop with the times. With these basic jazz dance steps as a foundation, you can explore creating your own walks and steps. Grooving to the music while executing the steps, footwork, and walks in jazz dance is one of the great joys of taking class. Next, you will explore turns you can add to your list of across-the-floor skills.

Turns

Building on the jazz dance turns done in the center, jazz dance turns across the floor include both those that travel through space and those that revolve around the body's own axis. The ability to spot well remains an important aspect of turning. To spot, you look at a place in space and hold that focus for as long as you can. When you can no longer maintain the spot, you whip the head around quickly and return to focus on the same place in space. The turning steps in this section are progressions that increase in complexity from one to the next.

Fred Astaire Turn

Fred Astaire turn: a small leap into a position with one leg behind and crossed over with the ball of the foot touching, both legs bent, and then turning toward the back leg while keeping the balls of both feet on the floor.

Self-Check

- After you have the feet, try adding arms. For example, open the arms to second position on the small leap. As you turn, bring the arms into first position.
- Make sure to spot the front while turning.
- Keep the knees bent during the turn and positions and travel sideways in the leap instead of up.

Chaînés

Chaînés: chains, links. A series of rapid turns moving in the same direction on the balls of the feet with the knees either bent or straight.

Self-Check

- Keep the arms quiet and still in a classical first position during chaînés turns.
- The feet should be only as far apart as a relevé in classical first position.
- Turn the entire half side of the body at once rather than taking steps.
- Use a sharp spot, looking over the shoulder of the lead foot as long as you can, even while stepping with the second foot. Then quickly whip the head around to find your spot before stepping down with the first foot.

Touch Turn

Touch turn: a turn to the outside done on the balls of the feet in which the free foot touches in back during the turn before stepping down fully on completion of the revolution.

Self-Check

- Be mindful of the tendency to put weight on the foot touching behind during the turn. The ball of the touching foot should use only enough weight to help maintain balance in the turn. As the step becomes more manageable, the weight in the touch decreases.

• Try a variety of arm positions for added challenge. For example, start with the arms in classical first, open to second on the step to the side, take the arm on the side of the leg doing the touch up to classical fifth on the touch, and close both arms to classical first on the step across.

Soutenu Turn

Soutenu turn: sustained turn. A smooth turn with both feet on the floor raised on the balls of the feet.

Self-Check

• Crossing the feet before beginning the turn creates a sustained moment facing front when done altogether.

• Try spotting front as well as to the side. The front makes a stronger statement visually, but at quicker tempos spotting in the direction of travel is helpful.

Pirouette

Pirouette: whirl or spin. A complete turn of the body on one foot raised on the balls of the feet. The other foot is commonly beside the knee, in a parallel or turned-out position of the leg. Also, pirouettes can be done turning away from the supporting leg or toward it.

Self-Check

• Use a clean, sharp spot.

• Be mindful that the ankle of the supporting leg, when high on the balls of the foot, remains properly aligned.

• Initiate the turn from the lower body, not the arms. Avoid the tendency to wind your arms in the opposite direction just before you begin to turn.

Compass Turn

Compass turn: a turn on one foot with the other leg held in any position, extended or bent, touching the floor.

Self-Check

• In the classical version, stay low with the knee bent and the toe of the extended leg tracing a circle on the floor.

• In a contemporary version, perform high on the balls of the feet and drag the toe close in to the supporting leg.

Pencil Turn

Pencil turn: a turn on one foot with the other leg held straight beside the turning leg.

Self-Check

- Use little energy to initiate this turn because the act of bringing the leg in to the center of the body creates more than enough momentum.
- Be mindful that the ankle of the supporting leg remains properly aligned.
- Try different arm positions like arms overhead with one hand grabbing the other wrist.

With the ability to perform turns across the floor that travel through space, like chaînés turns, and those that revolve around the body's own axis, like pirouettes, you have a wide range of challenging and interesting jazz dance skills. Whirling and turning in jazz dance is an exciting sensation. Next, you will explore steps that take you flying through the air and space in elevations.

Jump, Hop, and Leap Steps

Jump, hop, and leap steps done across the floor not only move through space but also combine with other elements, such as footwork, walks, and turns, to create challenging and exciting steps. You will find the rush from leaping and jumping through space one of the exciting and energizing aspects of jazz dance class. The elevation steps in this section are progressions that increase in complexity from one to the next.

Retiré Hop

Retiré hop: a hop in which the other foot is placed by the side of the knee (also called passé hop, passé sauté, retiré sauté).

Self-Check

- Stretch both feet in the air while bringing the thigh of the leg that has the foot by the knee parallel with the floor.
- To build momentum, start with a jazz chassé that travels across the floor.
- Try this step with a turned-out retiré.

Grand Battement Hop

Grand battement hop: a swing of the leg up to the front, side, or back while executing a hop on the standing leg. Can also be done to a tilt position.

Self-Check

- Make sure to brush the battement foot through tendu (a fully stretched leg and foot) on the way to the grand battement.
- Stretch both feet fully while in the air.
- Use correct placement of the leg and hips when doing it to the side.

Hitch Kick

Hitch kick: a leap onto one foot (which becomes the supporting leg) while doing a grand battement or flick kick with the free leg. Can be done front, side, and back (often done with a bent leg).

Self-Check

- Keep the spine long throughout the hitch kick.
- Make sure that the leap happens on the "and" count so that the height of the kick is on the beat.

Stag Leap

Stag leap: a forward leap in which the forward leg is in parallel retiré and the backward leg is straight.

Self-Check

- The momentum for the leap derives from the knee going into the retiré position and the back leg pushing off the floor.
- Make a picture in the air with one leg fully in retiré and the other extended behind before landing.

These jazz dance students are performing a stag leap where the front knee drives forward, propelling the body into the air.

Grand Jeté

Grand jeté: big thrown (step). A long horizontal jump, usually forward, starting from one leg and landing on the other.

Self-Check

- Make sure to begin with a grand battement.
- Keep both knees and feet fully stretched in the air.

Saut de Chat

Saut de chat (or developé grand jeté): a grand jeté in which the front leg begins bent and then extends in the air.

Self-Check

- At the peak of the saut de chat, the legs should be of equal height.
- Use the traveling steps before the saut de chat to move across the floor and then focus on going up, not forward, when performing the leap.

Drag Leap

Drag leap: a leap in any direction with the trailing foot dragging across the floor.

Self-Check

- Approach this as a grand jeté that never leaves the floor so that the energy and momentum really travels in the direction out, not up.
- Control of the descent is vital for safety. The knee should never actually touch the floor because the weight is held on a flat forward foot in the landing.
- Actively engage the core muscles to execute this step safely.

Clip Turn

Clip turn: A turning jump with both knees bent and lifted in front.

Self-Check

- The knees come sharply into the position in the air. Although the body is revolving in the air, the emphasis of direction should still be up, not around.
- Spot in the traveling direction of the step.
- Keep the shoulders down and point the feet while in the air.

Over the Top

Over the top: a hop with one leg over the other leg, which is extended, slightly off the ground, and crossing in front of the body.

Self-Check

- The leg in the air can lightly touch the floor in front, but do not put any weight on it during the hop.
- Think of taking the hip of the hopping leg up and over. This initiates the step from the center of gravity.

Leaping across the floor in jazz dance class creates a kinesthetic rush. The combination of grooving, whirling, and leaping skills brings a sensation that makes jazz dance infectious. Having soared above the floor, you will next explore skills that go down to it in floor work and inversions.

Floor Work and Inversions

Jazz dance not only moves across the floor and leaps above it but also goes down to it. Athletic jazz dance steps involve the dancer moving down to the floor and up out of it quickly, as well as inversions in which the dancer goes upside down. The floor work and inversion steps in this section are progressions that increase in complexity from one to the next.

Hinge on Knees

Hinge on knees: from a kneeling position, tilting backward while maintaining a long line from the crown of the head to the knees.

Self-Check

- Engage the abdominal muscles to support the lower back.
- Watch for the tendency to sit in the hip socket and break the line of the thigh, spine, and head.
- Work slowly to show control and strength.

Hinge to Knees

Hinge to knees: aligned from the hips to the crown of the head, tilting backward in a second position parallel with knees bent and lowering to a kneeling position.

Self-Check

- Carefully lower the knees to the floor. The greatest amount of effort happens in the last 2 inches (5 cm) before reaching the floor.
- Do not arch the back; keep the core muscles engaged and active to support the lower back.
- Experiment with the position of the head and the way in which it affects the hinge.

> **TECHNIQUE TIP**
>
> If you lean backward in the hinge and bend the knees deeply, you create a counterbalance that makes lowering to your knees easier than if you stay up. This may feel counterintuitive at first, but trust your body and find the point of counterbalance.

Spiral Descent

Spiral descent: starting in a forward lunge position, a descent to the floor with both feet remaining on the ground while turning in one direction to end in a seated pretzel position.

Self-Check

• Use your hands to help at first but then try to do it without them.

• Take this slow and work on doing the descent and ascent with control.

Seated Side Fall

Seated side fall: starting from a seated position on the heels, a descent to the floor ending on the side, giving the illusion of falling.

Self-Check

• Reach with the arm overhead to allow a controlled descent to the floor.

• Make the descent one smooth motion without any sound.

Side Fall

Side fall: a descent to the floor ending on the side, giving the illusion of falling.

Self-Check

• Reach with the arm overhead to create a counterbalance that will allow a controlled descent to the floor.

• Lowering to the back leg should be smooth and controlled, even when done fast.

• The direction is down and then out to the side.

Coffee Grinder

Coffee grinder: a floor move. In a squat on one bent leg, the other leg extended oscillates around in a complete circle and weight shift to the hands momentarily as the bent leg hops over the oscillating leg.

Self-Check

• Challenge yourself to keep the circling leg straight the entire time.

• This fun step builds upper-body strength that will aid in future steps. Notice the shifts of weight from one foot to both arms and back.

Jazz Back Fall

Jazz back fall: stepping back to a knee and continuing to lie back on the floor.

Self-Check

• Release into gravity and embrace the momentum.

• For a challenge, try this without the use of your arms.

Cartwheel

Cartwheel: an inversion in the vertical or door plane going onto one hand, then the other, and finishing on the opposite side.

Self-Check

• This is just one variation of the typical cartwheel. The details are not as important as summoning the courage to go fully upside down and gaining the strength in the arms to support the body.

• Learn to do this exercise on both sides. Most of us have a favorite side and need to be encouraged to try to master the other side.

• For added challenge, end the cartwheel standing on one leg.

Jazz Slide

Jazz slide: a slide into the floor with the front leg straight, back leg in attitude, and weight on the same hand as the front leg. Can end in a front split or a jazz split (back leg bent).

Self-Check

• Keep the energy of the jazz slide moving in the traveling direction.

• Make sure to put weight on the hand so that you create a tripod-like base with your body instead of dropping straight down into a split position.

These students are performing a jazz slide where the weight is distributed on three points (like a tripod) as they descend to the floor.

Floor work and inversions in jazz dance require you to have the courage to fall and the upper-body strength to support yourself when upside down. The ability to get into and out of the floor with dynamic energy makes jazz dance a physically demanding form of dance.

The athletic quality of jazz dance class, from the coordination in footwork, the whirling around, the leaping through the air, and the inversions from getting in and out of the floor, makes it both a physically strengthening and enjoyable dance form. With the skills worked on throughout the class, the next step is put all the steps together in a stylized combination in which you work on learning a small phrase of movement and dancing to the chosen music.

TYPES OF COMBINATIONS

Commonly, after executing the across-the-floor exercises, students in jazz dance classes learn and practice a combination. Combinations are small dances that allow students the opportunity to combine all the elements of the class, explore performance qualities and expression, develop artistry, and focus on a particular style. Some jazz dance teachers focus on their own personal style, whereas others teach a variety of styles. Types of jazz dance combinations include authentic jazz, musical theater jazz, African Caribbean jazz, classical jazz, modern jazz, street jazz, commercial hip-hop, lyrical jazz, and contemporary jazz.

Following the combination work, some type of cool-down usually follows, lasting about three to five minutes. The cool-down may be led by the teacher through a set exercise performed at the end of each class, or the teacher may improvise a cool-down while the students follow along. Alternatively, the teacher may let the dancers use the time to do their own cool-down. The cool-down signals the end of the class, lets the heart to return to its resting rate, and allows the dancers, teacher, and musician to pay respect to one another.

SUMMARY

A jazz dance class explores engaging skills and steps in the center, then across the floor, and finally in combinations. The kinesthetic rush from jazz dance, the enjoyment from moving rhythmically to the music, and the sense of community with your fellow dancers leaves you feeling alive and looking forward to the next class. An even greater appreciation and understanding about your experience in jazz dance class can come from learning about the rich history and legacy of this dance form. In the next chapter, you will learn about the characters, the trends, and the dances that went into jazz dance as you experience it today.

To find supplementary materials for this chapter, such as learning activities, e-journal assignments, and web links, visit the web resource at **www.HumanKinetics.com/BeginningJazzDance.**

WEB RESOURCE

Chapter 8

History of Jazz Dance

The rich history of jazz dance parallels the social, economic, and political history of the United States from the early 1900s to today. In this chapter you will learn how jazz dance grew from West African roots into an American performing art, supported along the way by a fascinating list of artists, dancers, and choreographers. In addition, learning about how to view jazz dance, about significant jazz dance works, and about the array of jazz dance forms and styles will add important context to your time in the studio, making it a more resonant and enjoyable experience. Understanding jazz dance history helps you realize the connections between the varied expressions that jazz dance takes, as well as the vital connections that exist between the figures, personalities, and every jazz dance student, including you.

DEVELOPMENT OF JAZZ DANCE AS A PERFORMING ART

Jazz dance emerged in the early 1900s. From roots in West African rhythms and dance, jazz dance developed in the United States first as social dance forms. It then became a commercially vibrant form of entertainment dance and grew into a uniquely American performing art.

Jazz Dance Roots

Although jazz dance is a performing art that sprouted from American soil, its roots (like those of jazz music) reach back to the continent of Africa. The syncopation, dynamic rhythms, grounded and earthy posture, and movement generating from the torso that are trademarks of jazz dance have their beginning in West African music and dance.

Understanding the history of jazz dance requires looking back to the 16th century and a terrible time in human history: the transatlantic slave trade. West African slaves working on plantations in the United States—removed from their homes, families, and rituals—shared their music and dance with each other. The music and dance of the West African slaves contrasted sharply with the European dances of the plantation owners. The West African dances and rhythms were a fascinating curiosity to white plantation owners.

White Americans appropriated the steps and music from the slaves, often performing them in caricature in minstrel shows. **Minstrel shows** were performances in the 19th century consisting of comic skits, music, and dance performed by white performers in blackface. The **cakewalk** was a popular dance tradition for slaves on plantations in the 19th century that was adopted by white performers and presented in minstrel shows.

By the early 20th century, the melding of the ritualistic and traditional music, rhythms, and movements from West African culture combined with Western European dance and music traditions. This mix created unique forms of vernacular, or popular, dance and music in the United States as people embraced the new rhythms and sounds.

Jazz Dance as Social Dance

Drawing from the African American experience, jazz dance originated as a social dance form in the early 20th century that accompanied the popular music of its time: jazz music. Although jazz dance has evolved since the early 1900s and now takes on many forms and styles, it continues to remain connected to the popular social dance forms of the day. The 1920s saw popular dance (jazz dance) crazes erupt with dances such as the Charleston and the black bottom. In the 1930s jitterbug and Lindy hop became popular. The 1940s saw the rise of swing, which later would undergo a renaissance in the 1990s. This tradition of jazz dance drawing from social dance forms continues through every decade. Social dance in the 21st century is dominated by hip-hop. Although hip-hop is commonly traced back to breaking, also called B-boying or break dancing, from the late 1970s, it follows the trend of social dances being connected to the music of the times, suggesting that hip-hop shares a history with jazz dance. Hip-hop has evolved into its own genre, but it has influenced commercial jazz dance styles that have taken the flavor of hip-hop steps and brought them into suburban and rural dance studios. An exploration of the social dance steps through the decades will help you see how popular trends in dance and music relate to jazz dance.

The Birth of Jazz

Dixieland jass (or jazz) music was the popular music in the early 1900s in New Orleans. The dancing that accompanied the popular music played in bars, night-clubs, and social situations was called freestyle or jass dance. This dancing marked the birth of jazz dance as well as the birth of the link between popular music and social dance forms that continues today.

> ### DID YOU KNOW?
>
> Jazz dance got its name as the social dance form done to the popular music in the early 1900s in New Orleans called jass (or jazz).

1920s: Jazz Age

In the 1920s two particular dance crazes emerged in social dancing and gained national attention: the Charleston and the black bottom. The **Charleston** was the most popular of 1920s dance crazes and an iconic symbol of the Jazz Age and flapper culture. The Jazz Age was a complicated but carefree time in United States culture. Excess and hedonism in high society mixed with women's breaking from the conventional norms of femininity. The stereotype of the new liberated woman, or flapper, cut her hair short, smoked long cigarettes, donned fringed dresses, and danced the Charleston with abandon. The Charleston became a staple of movie, musical, and even literary depictions of the Jazz Age. In *The Great Gatsby,* author F. Scott Fitzgerald portrayed the excessive and flapper-enthralled high society culture that thrived before the Wall Street crash of 1929.

Following the Charleston in popularity, the **black bottom** originated in New Orleans in the 1910s but did not become popular in nightclubs in Harlem, New York, until the early 1920s. It became a national craze in 1926. But after the Wall Street crash a few years later, popular dances like the Charleston and black bottom took a step back from the national limelight.

> ### ACTIVITY
>
> #### DO THE CHARLESTON
>
> With a partner, face each other and perform the Charleston. On the kick forward, touch your feet together. This partnered version of the Charleston became a popular step in the early 1990s named after a rap duo called Kid 'n Play.

1930s: Big Band Era

Although the Wall Street crash curtailed the popularity of mainstream social dance, social jazz dance and jazz music continued to develop in the dance halls in the 1930s, where African American dancers created new styles. Popular music changed from ragtime and Dixieland jazz of the preceding decades into big band music led by musicians such as Cab Calloway. Big band music, then and now, uses bold instrumentation and rhythmic syncopation that make it swing. The **big apple** is both a partner and circle dance created by African Americans to swing music in the 1930s that, in its form, draws comparisons to square dances. The **jitterbug** is a traditional jazz dance style from the 1930s done to big band music. It became popular in ballrooms such as the Savoy Ballroom in Harlem. The jitterbug was not a particular step, but a name for a whole style of social dancing. Movements included partnered and solo improvisations. Steps such as the Shorty George, truckin', Suzie Q, and crazy legs derive from the jitterbug style. **Lindy hop** is a partnered, athletic, and acrobatic traditional jazz dance style developed from the jitterbug in the 1930s and performed to big band music. Lindy hop got its name as a tribute to Charles Lindbergh, who became a celebrity after making the first solo flight across the Atlantic Ocean.

1940s: Swing Era, Authentic Jazz, and World War II

Interesting developments took place in the 1940s. As big band music continued to grow in popularity, Lindy hop became widespread. **Swing** dance is a partnered traditional jazz dance style derived from Lindy hop that entered mainstream American culture as a more moderate, less acrobatic version of partner dance done to big band music. At the same time that Lindy hop was spreading out and turning into swing, innovators in places like the Savoy Ballroom began exploring dance that they specifically called jazz. **Authentic jazz** is a highly individualized and syncopated traditional jazz dance style derived from early social jazz dance traditions such as the cakewalk, Charleston, black bottom, big apple, and Lindy hop.

DID YOU KNOW?

World War II greatly affected the evolution of jazz dance. Because many people had joined the war effort, jazz musicians were playing to near-empty houses. Jazz musicians therefore started to experiment with faster tempos and complicated melodic structures, which were difficult to dance to. In this moment of history, the link between jazz music and jazz dance broke.

As swing and authentic jazz were spreading, the affairs of the world at large interrupted when the United States entered World War II. Because many people had joined the war effort, jazz musicians were playing to near-empty houses. The expectation of getting audiences out of their seats and onto the dance floor faded. Jazz musicians therefore started to experiment. Through this experimentation the bebop era of jazz music emerged. Bebop, with its incredibly fast tempo and complicated melodic structure, was difficult to dance to. In this moment of history, the link between jazz music and jazz dance broke. Some jazz dance purists define jazz dance as the dancing that is done only to jazz music. From their perspective, dancing to other forms of music is not jazz dance. But when jazz music ventured into bebop, leaving social jazz dancing behind, jazz dance moved increasingly into Broadway musicals, into movie musicals, and eventually into dance studios, where it mixed with technical ballet training. The jazz dance popularized in dance studios across the United States would continue to be influenced by the social dance trends of the times.

1950s: Postwar Era

With World War II in the past, three significant innovations influenced the development of social dance: rock 'n' roll music, Latin dance, and television. Rock 'n' roll music stepped into the void of social dance music that jazz music left behind. The popularity of rock 'n' roll spread quickly, and sock hops became the social dance event for teenagers. The **sock hop** was an informal social dance gathering done in American high school gymnasiums in the 1950s to early rock 'n' roll music. The dancers had to remove their shoes to protect the gym floor. The dancing done to rock 'n' roll resembled an updated but tamer version of swing dance from the 1940s.

At the same time that rock 'n' roll had teens hopping, immigration from Central and South American countries to the United States brought with it Latin dance influences, such as the mambo. The **mambo** was the most popular Latin dance craze in the United States in the 1950s because of its sensual quality and rhythmic intricacy that reflected the influence of jazz music.

Both rock 'n' roll and the mambo spread across the country because of the growth of television. Shows like *American Bandstand* featured teenagers dancing to their favorite songs of the day. For the first time, social dance steps that used to be passed on through clubs, ballrooms, and movies were passed straight into American living rooms. Social dancing had changed dramatically in the 1950s because of the emergence of rock 'n' roll, and the ubiquity of television ensured that it would spread far and fast.

1960s: Dance Fads

The 1960s in America was a time of individuality mixed with mass commercialism. In social dance, partnering was out of fashion, leading to a multitude of individual social dance steps. The masses adopted these individual expressions of dance steps, and they became fads. **Fad dances** were widely popular dance crazes that appeared during the 1960s at incredibly frequent rates. Television and movies made the delivery of the latest and greatest fad easier and faster. These fad dances, including such steps as the twist, pony, monkey, mashed potato, and jerk, required no gender roles and no strict rules.

1970s: Disco and Street Dance

Disco was a trend in music and dance in the 1970s that featured complex partner and line dances done in nightclubs, or discotheques, complete with mirrored balls, strobe lights, and fog. Many disco dances required practice, and discotheques often held competitions.

Soul Train was a television show that began in 1971 and showcased teens dancing to popular soul and funk music. *Soul Train* introduced funk styles of dance, such as popping and locking, as well as breaking, to mainstream audiences and contributed to their popularity. **Popping** is a street dance style of funk dance from the West Coast that involves quick contractions and relaxations of the body. **Locking** has the same roots and involves freezing in the midst of quick movements and then continuing. It is characterized by large, exaggerated movement. **Breaking** (or B-boying), also called break dancing, is a street dance style that originated in New York City in the 1970s. It consists of top rock, down rock, power moves, and freezes. Popping, locking, and breaking are all associated with early hip-hop dance and culture.

1980s: Music Video Era

Music videos became popular in the 1980s with the creation of MTV, a television station dedicated solely to playing music videos. Popular (or pop) music before MTV relied on radio stations, albums, and concert tours to reach audiences. With the birth of MTV, pop musicians started to place more emphasis on the visual aspect of their acts, which often meant more dance. This shift coincided with characterizations of the 1980s as a surface- and image-focused time in American culture.

Although breaking flourished in the streets in the 1970s, it became a mainstream phenomenon in the early 1980s, appearing in movies, television shows, and music videos. The dynamic visual appeal of breaking's acrobatic feats made it a hit on the screen, where the flash and image of breakers captured people's attention.

By the mid-1980s, the popularity of breaking began to subside, and a flurry of new novelty dance fads came out of music videos to take its place. **Novelty fad dances** were dances of the mid- to late 1980s made popular by music videos and often named after pop culture items. Some popular steps included the running man, MC Hammer, the worm, Robocop, Cabbage Patch, Roger Rabbit, Reebok, the Kid 'n Play, and the moonwalk.

1990s: Vogue and Hip-Hop

Perhaps as a sign of social progression in America, social dance in the 1990s featured the mainstream acceptance of dance forms developed from historically marginalized groups: vogue and hip-hop. **Vogue** is a competitive dance form that came out of the gay ballrooms in Harlem, New York, and is characterized by model-like posing, stylized walking, and angular arm and leg movements. Vogue came into the mainstream through the success of the award-winning documentary *Paris Is Burning* in 1990 and a song and video by pop singer Madonna.

Hip-hop comprises a wide range of styles of dance that derive from hip-hop culture, including breaking, popping, and locking from the 1970s and Memphis jookin', terfing, and krumping in the 21st century. In the 1990s, hip-hop music, dance, and style gained mainstream popularity, not just as an independent trend but as its own popular culture. Although it went mainstream, hip-hop culture originated in marginalized communities of black and Latino youth.

The popularity of vogue and hip-hop in the 1990s paralleled changes in American culture in which issues of race and sexuality became national discussions that continued into the new millennium.

21st Century Social Dance

Social dance in the 21st century continues to follow the trends of the previous decades. Echoes of line dances, individual expression, societal events, fads, and cultural issues express themselves through the popular music and dance of the times. Whereas television, movies, and videos influenced social dance in past decades, the widespread growth of the Internet meant that popular dance could spread even faster and to even wider audiences, breaking down national barriers and reaching international viewers. Popular dance trends in the 21st century include the cha-cha slide, Harlem shake, lean wit it, chicken noodle soup, and the dougie.

Jazz dance as a social dance form attests to the power of music and movement as forms of self-expression. Rather than just being passing trends and fads, popular music and dance links directly to the heart and issues of a culture. These social dances not only reflect the times from which they come but also affect the entertainment and art of those decades and influence the times yet to come.

Jazz Dance as Entertainment

Beginning with vaudeville entertainment, social dance found its way to the stage. From vaudeville to Broadway to movies and television, the dynamic vitality of jazz dance and its ability to connect with the common person made it the most engaged form of dance in entertainment. **Vaudeville**, a type of theater popular in North America in the late 1800s and early 1900s, developed out of the minstrel shows and included several unrelated acts of music, comedy, magic, and dance. European dance of the time consisted mainly of early ballroom dance or ballet, which was used in early vaudeville. By comparison, social jazz dance in the early 1900s made for much more entertaining and accessible acts in vaudeville shows. The dynamic rhythms, accents, and footwork of social jazz dances were visually exciting and directly expressive for audiences to watch. Eventually, vaudeville developed into the form of entertainment we know as musical theater, which became a popular style of theater on Broadway and in movies and television. Movies made national celebrities out of dancers, perhaps none more so than Fred Astaire.

Fred Astaire (1899–1987) was an American movie and Broadway dancer, choreographer, singer, and actor whose performing career spanned 76 years. According to movie musical dancer Gene Kelly, "The history of dance on film begins with Astaire." Astaire trained in ballroom dance and tap but incorporated the syncopated rhythms and steps from jazz dance into his style.

Because choreographers wanted to use popular dances in movies, television, and on Broadway, they had to choose between using informally trained dancers from nightclubs who were experts in social jazz dance styles or formally trained ballet dancers who were unfamiliar with the nuances of the jazz steps. In the late 1940s dancer and choreographer Jack Cole persuaded the movie musical giant Columbia Pictures to give him time and space to train dancers specifically in this new style of movement for their movie musicals. The first formal training in theatrical jazz dance began under Cole's direction, opening the door for the growth of jazz dance as a theatrical dance form.

Jack Cole (1911–1974) was an American dancer, theater director, and choreographer who is considered the father of theatrical jazz dance. Early in his career, Cole danced with Ruth St. Dennis and Ted Shawn in the Denishawn Dance Company as well as with modern choreographers Doris Humphrey and Charles Weidman.

Although he started with modern dance, Cole went on to dance and choreograph for nightclubs, musicals, movies, and television. In the late 1940s he taught the first official jazz dance classes while

choreographing for Columbia Pictures after he convinced the company that the movie musicals they were producing would benefit if he were given the space and time to train the dancers in his acrobatic and angular style.

He went on to work with stars such as Rita Hayworth, Marilyn Monroe, and Gwen Verdon. His film work includes *Moon Over Miami*, *Cover Girl*, *The Merry Widow*, *Meet Me After the Show*, *Gentlemen Prefer Blondes*, *There's No Business Like Show Business*, *The I Don't Care Girl*, and *Les Girls*, and he directed or cho-

This photo shows Jack Cole demonstrating his trademark low-to-the-ground and athletic style.

reographed the stage musicals *Carnival in Flanders*, *Kismet*, *A Funny Thing Happened on the Way to the Forum*, *Donnybrook!* and *Man of La Mancha*.

Gene Kelly (1912–1996) was an American theatrical jazz dancer, actor, singer, film director, producer, and choreographer. His energetic and athletic dancing style combined with his charm made him a star in movie musicals. He is most known for his performance in *Singin' in the Rain*.

Michael Kidd (1915–2007) was an American movie and stage theatrical jazz dance choreographer. He was an innovator in making the dances integral to the plot of the story in movie and stage musicals. He is best known for choreographing the movie *Seven Brides for Seven Brothers* and was the winner of five Tony Awards and an honorary Academy Award.

Jerome Robbins (1918–1998) was an American theater and movie director and choreographer whose work has included everything from classical ballet to musical theater jazz dance. Besides once being the artistic director of the New York City Ballet, he also choreographed numerous successful Broadway shows, including *On the Town*, *The King and I*, *The Pajama Game*, *West Side Story*, and *Fiddler on the Roof*.

He codirected and choreographed the movie of *West Side Story* in 1956, for which he won an Oscar with Robert Wise for best director. In 1989 he created *Jerome Robbins' Broadway*, a retrospective of the greatest theatrical jazz dances of his career.

Significant Robbins Work: *West Side Story* *West Side Story*, conceived, choreographed, and codirected by Jerome Robbins, is a stage and movie musical that reimagines William Shakespeare's *Romeo and Juliet* in 1950s New York City. The dance scenes in *West Side Story* furthered the plot along significantly and with serious content, innovations that contrasted starkly to prior musicals in which dances tended to pause the story line and serve as light distractions.

> ### DID YOU KNOW?
>
> It is reported that Jerome Robbins tried to create animosity and antagonism between the actors playing the rival gangs in *West Side Story* by not allowing them to eat together or socialize with each other.

Peter Gennaro (1919–2000) was an American theatrical jazz dancer and choreographer who danced in the Broadway productions of *Kiss Me, Kate* in 1948 and *Guys and Dolls* in 1950. He was a member of the trio in Bob Fosse's "Steam Heat" in *The Pajama Game* in 1954. As a choreographer, he collaborated with Jerome Robbins on *West Side Story*. Although he is not credited, some claim that he choreographed the bulk of "America" and "Mambo" in *West Side Story*. He later won a Tony Award for Best Choreography for the musical *Annie* in 1977.

Chita Rivera (b. 1933) is an American singer, theatrical jazz dancer, and actor in musicals most famously known for originating the role of Anita in *West Side Story* on Broadway. She was the first Hispanic woman and Latino American to receive a Kennedy Center Honors award, and she received the Presidential Medal of Freedom in 2009.

Bob Fosse (1927–1987) was an American musical theater choreographer and director, screenwriter, and film director who is widely considered to be among the most innovative and influential musical theater choreographers of the 20th century. He won eight Tony Awards for Choreography, as well as one for direction. He was nominated for an Academy Award four times, winning for his direction of *Cabaret*.

Fosse developed a theatrical jazz dance style that included the use of turned-in knees, sideways shuffling, and rolled shoulders. A trademark of his work was his use of props such as hats, canes, chairs, and gloves. Some of his most popular works are *The Pajama Game* (featuring "Steam Heat") and *Chicago*.

Significant Fosse Work: *Chicago*   *Chicago*, cowritten, choreographed, and directed by Bob Fosse, is a 1975 musical satire about political corruption and criminal celebrity-hood that opened on Broadway. It is based on a play by the same name about a fascination that arose in the 1920s Jazz Age with homicides committed by women in Chicago.

Gwen Verdon (1925–2000) was a critically acclaimed theatrical jazz dancer on Broadway in the 1950s and '60s. Verdon began as an assistant to Jack Cole for five years. She taught dance to performers who eventually became stars, although she was relegated to taking small roles in movie musicals.

She got her big break when choreographer Michael Kidd cast her in Cole Porter's musical *Can Can* (1953). Verdon went on to win four Tony Awards in her career and was the muse for her second husband, Bob Fosse.

Michael Bennett (1943–1987) was an American musical theater director, writer, and theatrical jazz dance choreographer and dancer. He won 7 Tony Awards for his choreography and direction of Broadway shows and was nominated for 11 more. In 1976 he won the Tony Award for Best Direction of a Musical and the Tony Award for Best Choreography for *A Chorus Line*. Bennett created *A Chorus Line* based on a precedent-setting workshop process, which he pioneered. He also directed and choreographed *Dreamgirls*.

Significant Bennett Work: *A Chorus Line*
A Chorus Line, choreographed and directed by Michael Bennett, is a 1975 musical that later became a film. The storyline plays out at an audition for a Broadway musical and

This photo shows Gwen Verdon and Bob Fosse in rehearsal. Their partnership expanded beyond the stage and studio as they were married for a period of time.

explores the personalities and issues of chorus dancers. The musical was created by recording interviews with professional dancers and drawing inspiration from the interviews.

Susan Stroman (b. 1954) is an American choreographer and stage and movie director. The Broadway shows *Contact* and *The Producers* and the movie *Center Stage* are her most well-known works.

Significant Stroman Work: *Contact*   *Contact*, coconceived, choreographed, and directed by Susan Stroman, is a musical dance play that premiered on Broadway in 1999. It won the Tony Award for Best Musical in 2000 amid controversy because it contained no original music and no live singing.

Jazz dance continues to be the most common dance genre on Broadway and in movies, but as other forms of entertainment emerged, jazz dance evolved as well. Commercial music concerts consisting of rock 'n' roll, pop, and hip-hop music often use backup dancers to frame and highlight the vocalists. Commercial jazz dance is an entertaining and theatrical form of jazz dance that is popular in live music concerts and in television, in movies, and on the Internet. Professional commercial jazz dancers are hired in the expectation that they can display pyrotechnical technique from formal studio training along with fluency in the latest, and sometimes past, social dance styles. These same dancers became a staple of music videos beginning in the 1980s. Television shows have featured trained commercial jazz dancers not just as backup dancers but as featured acts in shows such as *Solid Gold* in the 1970s, *Star Search* in the 1980s, and *So You Think You Can Dance* in the 21st century.

Michael Peters (1948–1994) was an American choreographer who danced with Talley Beatty and Alvin Ailey. He is best known for his choreography work in the Michael Jackson videos *Thriller* and *Beat It* as well as Pat Benatar's *Love Is a Battlefield*. In 1982 Peters shared a Tony Award for Best Choreography with Michael Bennett for the Broadway musical *Dreamgirls*.

Michael Jackson (1958–2009) was an American singer-songwriter, actor, and dancer who contributed greatly to dance and music videos in the 1980s. His performance of the moonwalk at the Grammys in 1984 created a national dance craze.

Significant Jackson Work: *Thriller*   *Thriller*, choreographed by Michael Peters and Michael Jackson, is a song and music video by Michael Jackson from 1983 presented as a 13-minute feature. *Thriller* is responsible for propelling the popularity of dance in music videos in the 1980s.

Besides having a major role in movies, television, musicals, concerts, and videos, commercial jazz dance is the most popular form of dance in Las Vegas shows, cruise ship entertainment, and theme park live shows.

Jazz Dance as a Performing Art

Some choreographers and dancers thought of themselves as concert dance artists. They challenged the idea of jazz dance as merely social or merely entertaining. From these pioneers who saw the potential in jazz dance as a concert dance form parallel to ballet and modern dance, jazz dance as a performing art evolved (often called concert jazz dance). Influences included trends in modern art, postmodern art, and contemporary art.

Pioneers of Jazz Dance as a Performing Art

In the midst of the popularity of jazz dance as social dance and entertainment, a group of pioneering people introduced the idea of jazz dance as a performing art. Besides Jack Cole, who insisted that the rhythms and steps of jazz dance be something worth deep artistic inquiry and investigation rather than just titillating entertainment, these pioneering artists forged the way for jazz dance as a performing art.

Katherine Dunham (1909–2006) was an African American dancer, choreographer, songwriter, author, scholar, educator, anthropologist, and activist who engendered respect from her research and performances for the lineage of steps from West Africa, the Caribbean, and African American dance in the United States. Dunham danced in many Hollywood movies, maintained the Katherine Dunham Dance Company for more than 30 years, and was renowned throughout America, Europe, and Latin America for her work in the dance field. As a leader in the field of dance anthropology and ethno choreology, Dunham brought respect for the history of African and Caribbean influences on American modern dance and jazz dance. Both Peter Gennaro and Gus Giordano studied with Dunham.

Significant Dunham Work: *Cabin in the Sky*   *Cabin in the Sky* is a musical staged by ballet choreographer George Balanchine that premiered on Broadway in 1941 and featured Katherine Dunham and her entire dance company. *Cabin in the Sky* became a film in 1943 and was a breakthrough for the time for featuring an African American cast.

Pepsi Bethel (1918–2002) was a traditional jazz dancer, choreographer, and founding director of Pepsi Bethel's Authentic Jazz Dance Theater. Bethel began his career exploring jazz dance with the jitterbug and Lindy hop and in the Savoy Ballroom in Harlem. He danced with Mura Dehn Jazz Ballet before starting his own company in 1960. In 1969 his company was chosen by the United States State Department to perform as cultural emissaries in nine African countries. He was a passionate advocate of what he called authentic jazz dance and gave serious attention to the traditional social dance steps that evolved alongside jazz music. His legacy continues through the work of former Bethel dancer Karen Hubbard.

Eugene Louis Faccuito (aka Luigi) (1925–2015) was a classical jazz dancer and teacher who survived a near fatal car accident but was paralyzed down one side of his body. Luigi created his own stretching exercises and routines that helped him recover. Eventually, he gained enough strength and was cast in MGM's *On the Town*, starring Gene Kelly and Frank Sinatra. He went on to dance in more than 40 films, such as *An American in Paris*, *Annie Get Your Gun*, *Singin' in the Rain*, *The Band Wagon*, and *White Christmas*.

In 1956 Luigi moved to New York to perform on Broadway before dedicating himself to teaching and sharing the dance method he created for his recovery. Luigi's jazz dance style is characterized as smooth and lyrical.

Matt Mattox (1921–2013) was a protégé of Jack Cole. Mattox danced and choreographed on Broadway and most notably in movie musicals such as *Seven Brides for Seven Brothers*, *Yolanda and the Thief*, *The Band Wagon* (partnering Cyd Charisse), *Till the Clouds Roll By*, *Gentlemen Prefer Blondes*, and *There's No Business Like Show Business*.

Mattox is most known for bringing a strict technical approach to jazz dance. As a trained ballet dancer, Mattox created a jazz technique that is clean, angular, and powerful. His classes follow the progression of a ballet class and include challenging arm combinations. Mattox moved to France, founded his own concert jazz dance company, and continued to develop and codify his jazz dance technique.

Gus Giordano (1923–2008) was an American jazz dancer from St. Louis who performed on and off Broadway, in television, in movies, and on stage. He was a master teacher. He founded Gus Giordano Jazz Dance Chicago, created the Jazz Dance World Congress, and wrote the first book on jazz dance, *Anthology of American Jazz Dance*.

Giordano's style of jazz dance introduced modern dance elements into jazz, such as the use of contraction. Giordano Jazz Dance Chicago and the Jazz Dance World Congress

This photo shows Matt Mattox leaping on the movie set of *Seven Brides for Seven Brothers*, choreographed by Michael Kidd.

continue today under the direction of his daughter Nan Giordano.

These jazz dance artists, choreographers, and teachers were pioneers who, in their passion and respect for jazz dance, elevated the form to be taken seriously as an important art, rather than just a recreational activity.

Modern Influences on Jazz Dance

Jazz dance was born out of the modern industrial era in American history that spans from the late 1800s to around 1960. As a performing art form in modern society, influences from other cultures as well as modern artistic trends greatly influenced jazz dance during this period.

The investigation, largely because of Katherine Dunham, into West African and Caribbean culture, helped illuminate the rich history and tradition behind social jazz dance steps. Rhythms and footwork from social jazz dance steps trace back

The legacy of Katherine Dunham (pictured here) is carried on through the Katherine Dunham Centers for Arts and Humanities. Read more at kdcah.org.

to specific West African and Caribbean tribes and communities. This knowledge gave African American dancers a sense of tradition and history that had been lost because of the slave trade.

In addition, through the Caribbean tradition, Latin influences joined with social jazz dance, entertainment jazz dance, and jazz dance as a performing art. Although the mambo originally became a social dance craze, its rhythms and style showed up in dance done as entertainment and as art. Jazz dance as a performing art was also widely influenced by modern dance through choreographers such as Lester Horton, Alvin Ailey, and Talley Beatty.

Lester Horton (1906–1953) was an American modern dancer, choreographer, and teacher who worked in California choreographing for concert dance and movie musicals. Horton formed the Lester Horton Dancers in 1932. The company evolved through many name changes and appeared in films as the Lester Horton Dancers.

To finance his school and various dance companies, Horton choreographed movie musicals including *Moonlight in Havana* (1942), *White Savage* (1943), and *The Phantom of the Opera* (1943). Horton's student Alvin Ailey moved to New York City and spread Horton's dance technique to the East Coast. Horton-influenced jazz dance technique classes developed from Ailey's work in New York City.

Alvin Ailey (1931–1989) was an American dancer, choreographer, and founder of the Alvin Ailey American Dance Theater. Ailey popularized modern dance and African American participation in concert dance. Ailey studied and danced with Lester Horton in California before moving to New York City to dance on Broadway. For his dance company's inaugural concert in 1958, Ailey engaged fellow Broadway dancers.

Ailey's choreography mixed ballet, modern dance, jazz dance, and African dance techniques. His use of traditional jazz dance steps in a concert dance format was pivotal in the development of jazz dance as an artistic dance form.

Significant Ailey Work: *Revelations* *Revelations* by Alvin Ailey is the signature work of the Alvin Ailey American Dance Theater. It premiered in 1960 and draws on traditional jazz dance, modern jazz dance, and the modern dance technique of Lester Horton to explore the history of African Americans through spiritual and blues music.

Talley Beatty (1918–1995) was a dancer, educator, and company director. A student of Katherine Dunham and Martha Graham, Beatty went on to create choreography about the social issues, experiences, and everyday life of African Americans. Beatty's style was a mix between jazz and ballet that was often fast and explosive.

Many of Beatty's choreographic works were given a home in the repertory of the Alvin Ailey American Dance Theater. Beatty's use of social dance, jazz dance, and Dunham-influenced African and Caribbean dance fit well within Ailey's company.

Donald McKayle (b. 1930) is an American choreographer, director, teacher, and writer. He has created socially-conscious work for modern concert dance companies, and he choreographed and performed for Broadway musicals, television, and movies. He has been nominated for Tony and Emmy Awards.

Diane McIntyre (b. 1946) is an American dancer, choreographer, and teacher. McIntyre is known for her passion for exploring ways to move to live jazz music. Her company and studio, Sounds in Motion, was the only modern dance studio in Harlem in the 1970s and '80s. It served as a gathering place not only for dancers but also for musicians, scholars, and activists.

Daniel Nagrin (1917–2008) was an American dancer, choreographer, teacher, and author. He performed and choreographed on Broadway with his wife Helen Tamiris as well as in modern dance companies. Nagrin is known for incorporating jazz dance into his modern dance works.

Carmen De Lavallade (b. 1931) is an American dancer, choreographer, actor, and teacher. After dancing with the Lester Horton Dance Theater, she moved to New York City with Alvin Ailey. She has received many awards, including the Black History Month Lifetime Achievement Award, Rosie Award, Bessie Award, Capezio Dance Award, and an honorary doctor of fine arts from Juilliard.

During the modern industrial era in American history, the focus in modern art and modern dance on abstract shapes, technical achievement, skill of execution, and rational thematic content influenced modern concert jazz dance.

Postmodern Influences on Jazz Dance

The postmodern era in art, from the early 1960s to the 1990s, saw a leveling of the playing field between high (or formally trained) art and low (informally trained) art. An embrace of traditional, folk, and popular art as equal to the so-called high arts meant that in jazz dance, the hard line between social jazz dance, entertainment jazz dance, and artistic jazz dance faded. Three trends resulted. One trend brought renewed interest in social and entertainment forms as worthy of serious consideration as art in their own right. A second trend saw the growth of fusion dance styles in which individual teachers and choreographers mixed and matched their favorite elements to create their own hybrid, eclectic styles. The third trend, represented by teachers such as Lynn Simonson, drew from postmodern dance by introducing somatic (mind–body) practices, such as yoga, Laban movement analysis, Alexander technique, Feldenkrais method, and anatomically safe practices, into jazz dance.

The interest in traditional, social, and entertainment forms as art challenged the modern era superiority of high art. In the modern era, traditional or social jazz dance steps were absorbed into modern concert jazz dance with the unspoken message that they were being turned into art by this action. In the postmodern era, they were left whole and intact, celebrated without alteration.

This leveling of the playing field led dancers, choreographers, and dance companies to create fusion and collage styles by piecing together their personally favorite steps. For example, jazz dance choreographers fused West African dance with modern dance or jazz dance with ballet. Although proponents of these trends applauded the breaking down of the hierarchy of the high arts and individual innovation, detractors cautioned about the superficial, image-oriented, and fragmented focus of this period.

Mind–body practices such as yoga, Laban movement analysis, Alexander technique, and Feldenkrais method merged with jazz dance approaches in the work of teachers and choreographers, leading to anatomically safe jazz dance that carried less muscular tension and displayed more flow than it had in the past. These safer, flowing jazz dance techniques looked less dynamic than their percussive predecessors, but they introduced movement into jazz choreography that complemented it well.

Lou Conte (b. 1941) is an American theatrical jazz dancer, choreographer, and teacher who performed in Broadway musicals. He performed in the original cast of *How to Succeed in Business Without Really Trying* on Broadway at the age of 21. In 1972 he established the Lou Conte Dance Studio in Chicago. In 1977 he founded Hubbard Street Dance Chicago, which originally focused on combining ballet strength and discipline with jazz drive and showmanship by performing musical theater jazz dances in a dance concert format.

Danny Buraczeski (b. 1932) is an American dancer, choreographer, and classical jazz dance stylist. After a career on Broadway, Buraczeski formed his own classical concert jazz dance company, JazzDance, which he directed from 1980 to 2005. The company performed in more than 40 states as well as in Europe, Russia, and the Caribbean. He was the recipient of multiple grants from the National Endowment for the Arts.

Billy Siegenfeld is the founder and artistic director of Jump Rhythm Jazz Project in Chicago and the creator of jump rhythm technique. He is a strong advocate of using jazz music exclusively for jazz dance. He is the recipient of an Emmy Award, the Ruth Page Award, and the Jazz Dance World Congress Award for making "major contributions to the art of jazz dance." Besides choreographing and performing with his company, Siegenfeld is a Charles Deering McCormick Professor of Teaching Excellence at Northwestern University.

Lynn Simonson (b. 1943) is an American dancer and dance educator who trained in ballet but then started her career in musical theater. She moved to New York City at the age of 18 and danced with the Radio City Ballet Corps. Simonson was a student of Luigi. She was invited to teach in Holland in 1967, where she developed her own movement technique, Simonson technique, for jazz and modern dance.

Simonson experienced chronic injuries as a dancer that led her to develop a way of jazz dance training that was anatomically and kinesiologically sound as well as being independent of a particular style. Simonson technique is taught in 16 countries and is particularly popular in Japan, Holland, and Quebec.

Contemporary Influences on Jazz Dance

The contemporary (or transmodern) era of jazz dance as a performing art, from the 1990s into the 21st century, sees the development of artistic concepts that integrate elements of traditional, popular, modern, and postmodern trends. Contemporary art melds modern-era skill with postmodern-era innovation and variety. Contemporary concert jazz dance returns to the technical proficiency of the modern era but weds it with the diversity and flow from the postmodern era. Contemporary concert jazz dance continues to unfold, and it is as diverse as the many artists, dancers, and choreographers who are engaged in making it.

Rennie Harris (b. 1964) is a hip-hop dancer, choreographer, artistic director, and teacher who founded the hip-hop concert dance companies Rennie Harris Pure Movement and RHAW. He received honorary doctorates from Bates College and Columbia College. His company, RHAW, was chosen to serve as a cultural ambassador for President Obama.

Significant Harris Work: *Rome and Jewels*   *Rome and Jewels* by Rennie Harris is a work created in 2000. It was performed by his company, Rennie Harris Puremovement. *Rome and Jewels*, a hip-hop concert dance adaptation of William Shakespeare's *Romeo and Juliet*, is significant for bringing hip-hop dance and culture to the concert stage, crossing lines between social dance and art.

Mia Michaels (b. 1966) is an American contemporary jazz dance choreographer who grew up in Miami dancing at her family's dance studio. In New York City she received critical acclaim for her unique style of contemporary concert jazz dance and started her own company, RAW (Reality at Work), in 1997. During that time she also created work for Paper Mill Playhouse, Les Ballet Jazz de Montreal, Giordano Jazz Dance Chicago, and Oslo Dance Ensemble.

RAW folded, and Michaels left her work in concert jazz dance to focus on commercial work. Most notably, she choreographed for musical artists such as Celine Dion, Madonna, Ricky Martin, Gloria Estefan, and Prince. In 2005 she choreographed Cirque du Soleil's *Delirium*. In addition, she choreographed and judged for the television show *So You Think You Can Dance*.

From the pioneering vision of jazz dance artists who wanted the genre to be respected, jazz dance developed as a uniquely American performing art that now transcends national boundaries. Concert jazz dance draws together influences from trends in the art world with the rich tradition and history of a dance form born in the United States.

Jazz dance began as a social dance form in New Orleans that had roots reaching back to the west coast of Africa. As it developed and spread, it became a popular form in theatrical entertainments, first in live performances and now in television, in movies, and through the Internet. In the middle of the 20th century, it evolved into a distinctive artistic form.

JAZZ DANCE FORMS AND STYLES

Although the genre of jazz dance is commonly rhythm driven, in dialogue with gravity, directly expressive, and individualistic, there are many distinct forms and styles. Four major forms of jazz dance are traditional, theatrical, commercial, and concert. Within each form are a variety of styles, some crossing over from one form to the other. Recognizing the differences and similarities between the forms and styles will help you grow not only in appreciation but also in your ability to perform them in class.

Traditional Jazz Dance

The **traditional jazz dance** form (also called vernacular) consists of styles that derive from social dance trends and accompany jazz music. Traditional jazz dance styles originally came from the common people dancing in clubs or on the street, not from studio training.

Jitterbug

Jitterbug is a traditional jazz dance style from the 1930s done to big band music. It became popular in ballrooms such as the Savoy Ballroom in Harlem. The jitterbug was not a particular step, but a name for a whole style of social dancing. Movements included partnered and solo improvisations. Steps such as the Shorty George, truckin', Suzie Q, and crazy legs derive from the jitterbug style.

Lindy Hop

Lindy hop is a partnered, athletic, and acrobatic traditional jazz dance style that developed from the jitterbug in the 1930s and 1940s out of the Savoy Ballroom in Harlem, performed to big band music. Lindy hop got its name as a tribute to Charles Lindbergh, who became a celebrity after becoming the first person to fly solo across the Atlantic Ocean. The style consists of partnered and solo dances that incorporated traditional jazz dance steps and high-flying, acrobatic stunts. Sometimes used interchangeably with swing, Lindy hop refers specifically to the more acrobatic version from the 1930s. Swing refers to the more subdued, yet still athletic, mainstream version from the 1940s.

Swing

Swing dance is a partnered traditional jazz dance style derived from Lindy hop that entered mainstream American culture as a more moderate, less acrobatic version of partner dance done to big band music. In the 1990s swing underwent a renaissance and became socially popular again.

Authentic Jazz Dance

Authentic jazz dance is a highly individualized and syncopated traditional jazz dance style derived from early social jazz dance traditions such as the cakewalk, Charleston, black bottom, big apple, jitterbug, and Lindy hop. It is most often performed to jazz music from the ragtime, Dixieland jazz, Jazz Age, and big band swing eras.

Theatrical Jazz Dance

The **theatrical jazz dance** form (also called musical theater dance) consists of styles that derive from studio training and are performed on stage. Theatrical jazz dance styles emphasize presentation and incorporate traditional jazz dance styles with technical training in other forms, such as ballet, traditional African dance, or Caribbean dance. This form is found in Broadway musicals, movie musicals, and revues. Iconic choreographers for theatrical jazz dance include Jack Cole, Jerome Robbins, and Bob Fosse.

Jerome Robbins, shown here coaching dancers on the set of *West Side Story,* brought his pedigree in ballet to theatrical jazz dance.

Classical Jazz Dance

Classical jazz dance is a theatrical jazz dance style that emerged in the 1950s. It combined traditional jazz dance styles, developments in musical theater jazz dance, and ballet training. Jack Cole, Matt Mattox, Luigi, and Gus Giordano have created codified techniques of classical jazz dance. Classes are often highly structured and technical. Classical jazz dance appears in entertainment performances such as musicals as well as in concert dance performances.

African Caribbean Jazz Dance

African Caribbean jazz dance is a theatrical jazz dance style that incorporates African and Caribbean dance with traditional jazz dance. African Caribbean jazz dance was greatly influenced by the work of Katherine Dunham, who also presented this style as a concert jazz dance form. Classes in African Caribbean jazz dance often focus on rhythm and musicality. African Caribbean jazz dance is most often performed to African and Caribbean rhythms and music and appears in stage and movie musicals as well as in concert dance performances.

Musical Theater Jazz Dance

Musical theater jazz dance is a theatrical jazz dance style that joins the rhythm, weight changes, and steps from traditional dance with formal training techniques from ballet and classical jazz dance. Classes in musical theater jazz dance often focus on learning and performing dance scenes from musicals. Musical theater jazz dance is commonly found on Broadway, in movie musicals, and on live entertainment stages.

Commercial Jazz Dance

The **commercial jazz dance** form consists of styles that derive from studio training and often accompanies trends in popular music. Commercial jazz dance styles emphasize presentational and entertainment approaches that appeal to the masses and are responsive to the latest trends and fads in popular culture. This form is commonly found in Los Angeles and Las Vegas, at theme parks, on cruise ships, on television, in videos, in movies, and in the dance convention and competition circuit.

Street Jazz

Street jazz, also called jazz funk, is a commercial jazz dance style that incorporates street steps from hip-hop or novelty fad dances with dance studio training. Often characterized by stylized walks, head rolls, poses, snaps, and street steps merged with jazz dance technique turns, kicks, and leaps, street jazz is commonly found in dance studios and dance teams that compete with highly choreographed and synchronized routines. Classes are often high energy and focus on developing performance attitude alongside technique. Street jazz rose to popularity with the growth of dance conventions and competitions in the 1980s.

Lyrical

Lyrical is a commercial jazz dance style that became popular during the rise of dance conventions and competitions in the 1980s as a contrast to the percussive nature and fast tempo of jazz dance in studios. This recreational style of jazz dance includes flow, ballet-influenced movements, and strong dramatic content.

Commercial Hip-Hop

Commercial hip-hop is a commercial jazz dance style that is a dance studio version of hip-hop. It is commonly seen in backup dancers for singers and rappers in concerts and videos. Characterized as an urban social dance with studio technique, commercial hip-hop is hard hitting, heavily isolated, and performed with the feet firmly planted on the floor. The body is hunched forward in an aggressive posture and hanging loose. Unlike hip-hop, commercial hip-hop is often highly choreographed. Unlike street jazz, it does not highlight kicks, turns, and leaps.

Contemporary Commercial Jazz Dance

Contemporary commercial jazz dance is a commercial jazz dance style that integrates elements from contemporary dance practices, such as somatics and inversions, with the presentational qualities of jazz dance, often contrasting between moments of flow and isolation. It is found in dance competitions, conventions, and television shows, where it is sometimes called contemporary dance, causing confusion with contemporary concert dance.

Hip-Hop

Hip-hop began as a street dance style that developed similarly to traditional jazz dance styles. It then intersected with commercial jazz dance styles before developing into its own genre of dance. The name is given to a wide range of street dance styles derived from hip-hop culture, including breaking, popping, locking, Memphis jookin', turfing, jerkin', and krumping. Hip-hop dance is highly improvisational and competitive, characterized by crews, battles, and free styling. Hip-hop differs from street jazz and commercial hip-hop in that it does not include studio dance technique, highly organized choreography, or unison work.

Concert Jazz Dance

The **concert jazz dance** form consists of styles that derive from highly technical studio training and parallel classical ballet, modern dance, postmodern dance, and contemporary dance in their choreographic approach. Concert jazz dance styles emphasize artistic intent in choreography and performance, placing less emphasis on entertaining and more emphasis on making an artistic statement. This form is commonly found on stages in dance concerts presented by professional dance companies.

Classical Concert Jazz Dance

Classical concert jazz dance is a concert jazz dance style that emerged in the 1950s from theatrical jazz dance forms being presented on concert stages. When choreographers such as Jack Cole, Matt Mattox, Luigi, Gus Giordano, Katherine Dunham, and Pepsi Bethel presented their theatrical jazz dance forms as a performing art, their works were reframed from being theatrical entertainments to works of artistic expression. Classical concert jazz dance continued to develop past the 1950s in the works of groups and artists that include the American Dance Machine, Lou Conte, and Danny Buraceski.

Modern Concert Jazz Dance

Modern concert jazz dance is a concert jazz dance style characterized by a focus on shape, technical achievement, performing barefoot, and rational, abstract thematic content. As a style, modern concert jazz dance is typically performed barefoot, uses contractions, and engages work on the floor. Horton-based jazz technique classes are commonly found in New York City and Los Angeles. Modern concert jazz dance appears most often in concert jazz dance companies and in the repertory of modern dance companies.

Contemporary Concert Jazz Dance

Contemporary concert jazz dance is a concert jazz dance style focused on artistic expression that integrates elements from postmodern and contemporary dance practices, such as somatics and inversions, with the qualities of jazz dance, often contrasting between moments of flow and isolation. Contemporary concert jazz dance appears as technical and dynamic work in jazz, modern, and contemporary dance companies.

Jazz dance forms and styles continue to develop and change with the times. They appear as a sign of the times and simultaneously influence the future of jazz dance as a genre. Because of the inherent nature of jazz dance to continue to progress and change, as soon as a list of styles is made, it becomes obsolete. Already, new trends in music, popular culture, and national events conspire to bring about the next jazz dance style.

VIEWING JAZZ DANCE PERFORMANCES

Jazz dance appears on entertainment stages, artistic concert stages, in musicals, in movies, on television, and through the Internet. Knowing the etiquette for viewing live performances and the elements to look for in the performance helps you get the most out of the experience while also respecting the dancers and fellow audience members.

Live Performance Etiquette

When viewing jazz dance in the comfort of our homes on television or our Internet devices, we can relax and enjoy it any way we want. But when viewing live performances, certain expectations in etiquette serve to make sure that we display respect toward both the performers and other audience members. We have become a culture familiar with consuming experiences in front of computer screens that do not care whether we sing along, pause and restart, or multitask. Technological performances are different from human performances; a live performance has a different energy and a different set of appropriate behaviors.

Plan to arrive 30 minutes before the performance to offset unforeseen circumstances that might make you late. Arriving late to a live performance disrupts the experience for the dancers on the stage and the audience members who have arrived on time and have begun to enjoy the theatrical experience. If you arrive late, wait outside the theater until a break occurs between pieces. An usher will let you know when it is appropriate for you to enter and take your seat.

During the performance, any type of noise making or visually distracting device ruins the experience for the audience and performers. Before the start of the performance, turn off all devices that might make noise and do not check them during the performance. Although texting might seem unobtrusive to you, the people sitting around you may be distracted by such behavior and the glow from the screen in an otherwise darkened space can take audience members out of the magic of the theatrical moment. Also, any type of chatting, even whispering, to those next to you detracts from the experience.

Remain seated throughout the performance, getting up only during designated intermissions when the lights come up. For reasons mentioned before, entering and exiting during a performance distracts the performers and audience and is considered highly impolite.

Competitive dance on screen has created confusion about etiquette in a dance performance. Because the shows on television work to manufacture the excitement and energy of a live performance while you sit at home, they coach their audiences (or use prerecorded sounds) to behave like sports fans. These audiences cheer and clap for every impressive step and shout out encouragement. But these behaviors are incorrect for live dance performances. In a live jazz dance performance, etiquette commonly means that you wait for the end of a section or dance before applauding. If the performance is good and you are inspired, applaud vigorously, but not in the middle of a performance.

After the performance, the dancers often take a curtain call or bow. At this time you can applaud. Traditional displays of admiration include shouting, "Bravo." Contemporary displays in America include shouting, "Woo." Depending on the audience, both may be appropriate. But yelling names or behaving in ways typical of sporting events is frowned on.

Understanding the Choreographer's Intent

When viewing jazz dance, whether on a screen or live, knowing basic elements of what to look for informs your experience. You will benefit by being able to understand the choreographer's intent, evaluate the dancers' skill, and consider the production elements that work in synergy to make the performance come to life.

Jazz dance choreographers can vary in their intent in making jazz dance. Some consider it art, some consider it entertainment, and most consider it a combination of both. Sometimes the choreographers want to relay a story, and sometimes they just want to explore a movement theme without a story. When watching jazz dance, consider the choices the choreographer makes. A particular choice to do a step might come from the intent to impress or excite the audience rather than something that is consistent to the prior steps of the dance. This choice suggests that the choreographer places priority on creating work that entertains the audience. Another choreographer might make a choice that comes from the intent to make a pleasing and consistent work rather than to excite or impress. This choice suggests that the choreographer places priority on creating an artistic statement. Sometimes, the choice appears consistent, pleasing, exciting, and impressive.

Jazz dances appear as narratives or abstract dances. Narrative dances relay a story, and the structure of the dance helps convey that story. Abstract dances do not tell a literal story. Instead, they focus on thematic elements that are developed and explored. Narrative dances convey a message or story with differing degrees of detail. Some you get right away, and others make you think and struggle to understand. Abstract dances convey an essence, not a message. Instead of trying to understand the message of an abstract dance, you should simply enjoy the experience of watching it.

Skill of Execution

The skill of the performers' technique, expression, and artistry affects your experience of a dance. Technique is the ability for a dancer to execute particular steps with accuracy and precision. Expression is the ability to express a mood or emotion in performance. Artistry is the ability to perform with style, nuance, and sensitivity. A dancer who performs with excellent accuracy and precision but poor emotion and sensitivity does well with technique, but not with expression or artistry. Likewise, a dancer who performs passionately but lacks precision and nuance does well with expression, but not with technique or artistry. Dancers work hard to bring these three elements of execution skill—technique, expression, and artistry—together in performance.

Production Elements

Besides the choreographer's and dancers' skill, production elements add to the performance experience. Choices in the use of set pieces, lights, costumes, and music work together to create the overall experience.

Set pieces can be literal, like a table and chairs in a restaurant scene, or abstract, like a large black wooden box. They help create an atmosphere for the dance and can even play critical roles in the choreography.

Lighting choices not only illuminate the dancers' bodies but also set a mood and texture for the piece. Lighting can be used subtly to set an atmosphere or dynamically, changing quickly and boldly, to interact with the dance.

Costumes can help convey a character, be used to reveal the form of the body, or be chosen for the movement quality that the material brings to the dance. Costumes often clue the audience about whether the dance is narrative, meant to portray particular characters of a story, or abstract, meant to serve a theme.

The relationship between music and dance, especially jazz dance, is often the strongest and most obvious of the production elements. Movement can interact in a parallel fashion with the music, in which the movement matches the music, or it can provide a counterpoint, in which the movement works in contrast to the music for effect.

The production elements of sets, lighting, costumes, and music join with the movement and dancers to create a fully realized piece of choreography. The choreographer's choices in both how to use and when not to use these elements make strong personal statements about the theme or narrative of the dance.

The combination of the choreographer's intent, the dancers' skill of execution, and the production elements of sets, lights, costumes, and music makes up the entire theatrical experience that goes into a jazz dance. You draw your own opinions based on whether you appreciate those elements individually or enjoy the experience as a whole.

As you are viewing and evaluating your experience of a live jazz dance performance, you are also part of that experience. Your understanding of etiquette and display of respect for the dancers and other audience members contribute to the total experience of all those participating in that performance, both performers and audience members.

SUMMARY

Now you have explored the history and variety of jazz dance forms and styles, from its development as social dance, entertainment, and art to its important artists and choreographers. You have learned about viewing jazz dance, some of the significant works of jazz dance, and the array of forms and styles that exist. And you know that the story of jazz dance is not complete. It is not simply in the past. It is alive here and now, and you are part of it. Whether you are a student, a performer, a teacher, or a choreographer, you contribute to jazz dance every time you take a class, watch a performance, or get up and dance.

To find supplementary materials for this chapter, such as learning activities, e-journal assignments, and web links, visit the web resource at www.HumanKinetics.com/BeginningJazzDance.

 **WEB RESOURCE**

Glossary

Achilles tendinitis—Inflammation of the Achilles tendon or its covering.

aerobic fitness—Associated with moderate, long-term levels of activity.

affirmations—A sport psychology technique that creates necessary confidence.

African Caribbean jazz dance—A theatrical jazz dance style incorporating African and Caribbean dance with traditional jazz dance.

agonist muscles—Muscles that contract to produce movement.

alignment—The organization of body parts in relationship to each other.

anaerobic fitness—Associated with high-intensity, maximal, short bursts of activity.

ankle sprain—An injury to the ligaments surrounding the ankle.

antagonist muscles—Muscles that oppose the primary movers.

attentive repetition—Working with full mental focus on a skill repeatedly by finding deeper layers of challenge.

authentic jazz dance—A highly individualized and syncopated traditional jazz dance style derived from early social jazz dance traditions such as the cakewalk, Charleston, black bottom, big apple, jitterbug, and Lindy hop.

axial movement—Action organized primarily around the axis of the spine and in relatively stationary space.

ball-and-socket joint—Consists of a bone with a rounded end meeting up with a cup-shaped bone, allowing a circular range of motion.

beat—The regularly occurring pulse of the music.

Bethel, Pepsi (1918–2002)—A traditional jazz dancer, choreographer, and founding director of Pepsi Bethel's Authentic Jazz Dance Theater.

big apple—A partner and circle dance created by African Americans to swing music in the 1930s that, in its form, draws comparisons to square dances.

black bottom—A dance that originated in New Orleans in the 1910s, became popular in nightclubs in Harlem, New York, in the early 1920s, and became a national craze in 1926.

body-half connectivity—The relationship between one side of the body and the other.

body shape—The overall structure of the body during a single step or string of steps.

breaking (also called B-boying or break dancing)—A street dance style that originated in New York City in the 1970s and consists of top rock, down rock, power moves, and freezes.

breath connectivity—The relationship between breathing and movement.

cakewalk—A popular dance tradition for slaves on plantations in the 19th century that was appropriated by white performers and presented in minstrel shows.

causal body—The part of being aware of the present moment by being centered, focused, and mindful.

centering—The process of focusing the mind.

cervical spine—The top seven vertebrae.

Charleston—The most popular of 1920s dance crazes and an iconic symbol of the Jazz Age and flapper culture.

classical concert jazz dance—A concert jazz dance style that emerged in the 1950s from theatrical jazz dance forms being presented on concert stages.

classical jazz dance—A theatrical and concert jazz dance style that emerged in the 1950s and combined traditional jazz dance styles, developments in musical theater jazz dance, and ballet training.

Cole, Jack (1911–1974)—An American dancer, theater director, and choreographer considered the father of theatrical jazz dance.

commercial hip-hop—A commercial jazz dance style that is a dance studio version of hip-hop.

commercial jazz dance—A form of jazz dance that consists of styles that derive from studio training and often accompanies trends in popular music.

combination—An extended movement sequence that combines the skills being worked on in class and explores specific stylistic and performance aspects of jazz dance.

compression (for injuries)—Application of an elastic compression bandage to the injured area.

concentric contraction—A shortening of the muscle to create movement.

concert jazz dance—A jazz dance form consisting of styles that derive from highly technical studio training and parallel classical ballet, modern concert dance, and contemporary concert dance in their aesthetic approach.

conditioning—A sequence of movements, usually done on the floor, that develop muscular strength, muscular endurance, and flexibility.

connected breathing—A subtle ensemble skill that helps with spacing, flocking, and timing.

connectivity—The pattern of relationship between body parts.

contemporary commercial jazz dance—A commercial jazz dance style that integrates elements from contemporary dance practices, such as somatics and inversions, with the presentational qualities of jazz dance, often contrasting between moments of flow and isolation.

contemporary concert jazz dance—A concert jazz dance style focused on artistic expression that integrates elements from postmodern and contemporary dance practices, such as somatics and inversions, with the qualities of jazz dance, often contrasting between moments of flow and isolation.

cool-down—A sequence at the end of class designed to slow the heart rate and gently stretch the muscles that have been worked, relieving excess tension.

coordination exercises—Exercises performed to integrate isolated body parts while developing correct posture, coordination of leg and arm movements, and articulation of the feet and ankles.

core-distal connectivity—The relationship between the muscles of the torso as they support and provide stability for the limbs in space.

cross lateral connectivity—The relationship between diagonally opposing parts of the body.

deliberate practice—Working on technique just beyond grasp, seeking constant critical feedback, and focusing on strengthening weaknesses.

direct space—Specific and exact use of shape, pathway, and focus.

disco—A trend in music and dance in the 1970s that featured complex partner and line dances done in nightclubs, or discotheques, complete with mirrored balls, strobe lights, and fog.

downstage—Toward the audience or front of the studio.

Dunham, Katherine (1909–2006)—An African American dancer, choreographer, songwriter, author, scholar, educator, anthropologist, and activist who engendered respect from her research and performances for the lineage of steps from West Africa, the Caribbean, and African American dance in the United States.

dynamic contraction—The length of muscle changes.

eccentric contraction—A lengthening of the muscle to create movement.

effort actions—The combination of one element of space (either direct or indirect) with one element of time (quick or sustained) with one element of weight (strong or light).

elevation (for injuries)—Raising of the body part above the heart.

endurance—The ability to produce continuous movement through muscular and cardiovascular conditioning.

Faccuito, Eugene Louis (aka Luigi) (b. 1925)—A classical jazz dancer and teacher who survived a near fatal car accident but was paralyzed down one side of his body.

fad dances—Widely popular dance crazes that appeared during the 1960s at incredibly more frequent rates.

feel it from inside—A process that includes setting a goal, reaching for it, evaluating the attempt, and repeating the cycle.

flexibility—The range of motion at a joint in association with the pliability of a muscle.

flocking—The ability to adapt movement spontaneously while also maintaining spacing.

flow—A state of optimal inner experience characterized by absorption in the moment from the merging of action and awareness.

focus—Orientation of attention to the surrounding space.

follow-through—The residual movement after the main action.

forward pelvic tilt—The top of the pelvis moves forward of the centerline of the body while the bottom of the pelvis moves behind the centerline of the body.

general space—The space of the studio or stage.

Giordano, Gus (1923–2008)—An American jazz dancer from St. Louis who performed on and off Broadway, in television, in movies, on stage, and as a master teacher.

gliding joint—Consists of two bones meeting up with mostly flat surfaces.

gross body—The part of a person's being made of physical muscles and bones.

head-tail connectivity—The relationship between the crown of the head and the tip of the tailbone.

hinge joint—Consists of a bone with a slight concave end meeting up with a bone with a slight convex end, allowing primarily for extension and flexion.

hip-hop—A wide range of styles of dance that derive from hip-hop culture, including breaking, popping, and locking from the 1970s and Memphis jookin', terfing, and krumping in the 21st century.

hyperextension—The ability of a joint to go beyond extension.

hyperlordosis—An exaggeration of a secondary curve of the spine.

ice (for injuries)—Application of ice to the injured area.

indirect space—Nonspecific and general use of shape, pathway, and focus.

initiation—How the movement begins.

inner initiation—Movement that begins from a central point in the body and moves outward.

intonation cues—The use of pitch in delivery of words or sounds to convey information about movement.

impact—Phrasing that starts easy and slow but speeds up and gets stronger along the way until you reach full speed and strength at the end of the movement.

impulse—Phrasing that starts with a pulse of energy but then gradually fades away.

isolations—A series of exercises that mobilize one body part at a time to develop refined, specific control.

jitterbug—A traditional jazz dance style from the 1930s done to big band music that became popular in ballrooms such as the Savoy Ballroom in Harlem.

joints—The place where two or more bones interact.

jumper's knee—An injury to tendons around the knee characterized by an aching feeling.

kinesiology—The science of human motion.

kinesthetic sense—The awareness of the body and movement ability.

kinesthetic sensing—The ability to feel the position of the body and limbs in space.

Lindy hop—A partnered, athletic, and acrobatic traditional jazz dance style developed from the jitterbug in the 1930s and 1940s out of the Savoy Ballroom in Harlem and performed to big band music.

locking—A street dance style of funk dance from the West Coast that involves freezing in the midst of quick movements and then continuing, characterized by large, exaggerated movement.

locomotive movement—Action organized primarily around the task of changing location in space from one place to another.

lumbar spine—The five vertebrae below the thoracic vertebrae.

lumbosacral strain—An injury to the small extensor muscles or ligaments of the spine.

lyrical—A commercial jazz dance style that became popular during the rise of dance conventions and competitions in the 1980s as a contrast to the percussive nature and fast tempo of jazz dance in studios.

mambo—The most popular Latin dance craze in the United States in the 1950s because of its sensual quality and rhythmic intricacy that reflected the influence of jazz music.

marking—To do a movement or step with reserved energy and use of space.

Mattox, Matt (1921–2013)—A protégé of Jack Cole, most known for bringing a strict technical approach to jazz dance.

mechanical low back pain—A condition involving localized lower back pain.

minstrel shows—Performances in the 19th century consisting of comic skits, music, and dance performed by white performers in blackface.

modern concert jazz dance—A concert jazz dance style characterized by a focus on shape, technical achievement, performing barefoot, and rational, abstract thematic content.

musical theater jazz dance—A theatrical jazz dance style that joins the rhythm, weight changes, and steps from traditional dance with formal training techniques from ballet and classical jazz dance.

novelty fad dances—Dances of the mid- to late 1980s made popular by music videos and often named after pop culture items.

observation skills—Three learning modalities of aural (listen), visual (watch), and kinesthetic (do).

outer initiation—Movement that begins from the outer edges of the body or from the environment and moves toward the center.

pathway—Route the body takes between shapes.

percussive—Phrasing that is precise and sharp and works well in synchronized movement.

personal space—The area surrounding the dancer, including the distance between the dancer and others.

plane—An imaginary flat surface that passes through the body.

popping—A street dance style of funk dance from the West Coast that involves quick contractions and relaxations of the body.

power—The explosive (speed-related) aspect of muscular strength.

primary curves—Spinal curves that are concave, hollowing out toward the front of the body.

progression—A series of exercises performed moving across the floor that incorporates learned movement vocabulary with a focus on traveling through space from one point to another.

pronation—The ankles rolling in toward the centerline of the body.

protection (for injuries)—Removing additional danger or risk from the injured area.

recalling—A sport psychology technique that mentally prepares a person for positive performance experiences by remembering past successes.

rest (for injuries)—Cessation of dancing and moving the injured area.

rhythmic cues—The patterned delivery of words or sounds to convey information about movement.

secondary curves—Spinal curves that are convex, bulging out toward the front of the body.

sequence—Order in which movements occur.

sequential sequence—Movement that follows one after the other in nonadjacent body parts.

shape—Position of the body in space.

shifting transition—Abrupt movement changes from one step to the next.

shin splints—A condition in which the dancer feels tenderness and discomfort on the front of the shin, especially when jumping.

simultaneous initiation—Body parts all beginning to move at once.

simultaneous sequence—Movements occurring at the same time.

sinking hip—Moving the pelvis off center and shifting body weight more toward one side.

sock hop—An informal social dance gathering done in American high school gymnasiums in the 1950s to early rock 'n' roll music in which the dancers had to remove their shoes to protect the gym floor.

spacing—The position within a group that a dancer must maintain, requiring an understanding of personal space as it relates to general space.

spatial sense—An awareness of space and the way in which objects, including the self and others, occupy space.

stage left—From the viewpoint of the dancer onstage facing the audience or in the studio facing the front, to the dancer's left.

stage right—From the viewpoint of the dancer onstage facing the audience or in the studio facing the front, to the dancer's right.

street jazz (also called jazz funk)—A commercial jazz dance style that incorporates street steps from hip-hop or novelty fad dances with dance studio training.

strength—The ability for the muscle to produce maximal force on one occasion.

subtle body—The part of a person's being that senses inner energy fluctuations and neuromuscular connectivity.

successive sequence—Movement that follows one after the other in adjacent body parts.

supination—The ankles rolling out from the centerline of the body.

swing (dance)—A partnered traditional jazz dance style derived from Lindy hop that entered mainstream American culture as a more moderate, less acrobatic version of partner dance done to big band music.

swing (phrasing)—Phrasing that oscillates between moments of full release and moments of suspension.

syncopation—The placing of an accent unexpectedly on the upbeat rather than the downbeat.

theatrical jazz dance—Also called musical theater dance, consists of styles that derive from studio training and are performed on stage.

thoracic spine—The next 12 vertebrae below the cervical spine.

traditional jazz dance (also called vernacular)—A form of jazz dance consisting of styles that derive from social dance trends and accompany jazz music.

transformational transition—One step gradually evolving into the following one.

transition—A follow-through that connects one movement to the next.

tucking under—The bottom of the pelvis rounding forward and under.

upper-lower connectivity—The relationship between the lower body (hips and legs) and the upper body (torso and arms).

upstage—Toward the back of the stage or studio.

vaudeville—A type of theater popular in North America in the late 1800s and early 1900s that developed out of minstrel shows and included several unrelated acts of music, comedy, magic, dance, and other variety arts.

vibratory—Phrasing that alternates in quick, rapidly changing patterns.

visualization—A mental preparation technique that uses the imagination to prepare the neuromuscular connection for upcoming tasks.

vocabulary cues—The names of steps and movement techniques used for instruction.

vogue—A competitive dance form that came out of the gay ballrooms in Harlem, New York, and was characterized by model-like posing, stylized walking, and angular arm and leg movements.

warm-up—A series of exercises performed at the beginning of the class to awaken the body by getting blood flowing to all the major muscle groups of the torso, legs, and arms.

References and Resources

Clarkson, P. (2003). *Fueling the Dancer.* International Association for Dance Medicine and Science.

Clippinger, K.S. (2016). *Dance Anatomy and Kinesiology.* 2nd ed. Champaign, IL: Human Kinetics.

Coyle, D. (2009). *The Talent Code: Greatness Isn't Born. It's Grown. Here's How.* New York: Bantam Dell.

Csikszentmihalyi, M. (1990). *Flow: The Psychology of Optimal Experience.* New York: HarperCollins.

Delamater, J. (1981). *Dance in the Hollywood Musical.* Ann Arbor, MI: UMI Research Press.

Emery, L.F. (1988). *Black Dance: From 1619 to Today.* Pennington, NY: Princeton Books.

Ericsson, K. (2006). The influence of experience and deliberate practice on the development of superior expert performance. In *Cambridge Handbook of Expertise and Expert Performance.* http://library3.webster.edu/login?url=http://search.credoreference.com.library3.webster.edu/content/entry/cupexpert/the_influence_of_experience_and_deliberate_practice_on_the_development_of_superior_expert_performance/0.

Fitt, S.S. (1988). *Dance Kinesiology.* New York: Schirmer Books.

Franklin, E. (2014). *Dance Imagery for Technique and Performance.* 2nd ed. Champaign, IL: Human Kinetics.

Frich, E. (1983). *The Matt Mattox Book of Jazz Dance.* New York: Sterling.

Gallafent, E. (2000). *Astaire and Rogers.* New York: Columbia University Press.

Giordano, G. (1978). *Anthology of American Jazz Dance.* Evanston, IL: Orion.

Grubb, K.B. (1989). *Razzle Dazzle: The Life and Works of Bob Fosse.* New York: St. Martin's Press.

Hackney, P. (2002). *Making Connections: Total Body Integration Through Bartenieff Fundamentals.* New York: Routledge. (Original work published 1998.)

Hubbard, K.W. (2008). Valuing cultural context and style: Strategies for teaching traditional jazz dance from the inside out. *Journal of Dance Education.*

Jacob, E. (1993). *Dancing.* New York: Variety Arts.

Lihs, H.R. (2002). *Appreciating Dance: A Guide to the World's Liveliest Art.* Highstown, NJ: Princeton Book.

Loney, G. (1984). *Unsung Genius: The Passion of Dancer-Choreographer Jack Cole.* New York: Franklin Watts.

Long, R.E. (2001). *Broadway, The Golden Years.* New York: Continuum.

Perces, M., Forsythe, A.M., and Bell, C. (1992). *The Dance Technique of Lester Horton.* Pennington, NJ: Princeton Book.

Sefcovic, N. (2010). *First Aid for Dance.* International Association for Dance Medicine and Science.

Siegenfeld, B. (2009). Standing down straight: Jump rhythm technique's rhythm-driven, community directed approach to dance education. *Journal of Dance Education.*

Stearns, M., and Stearns, J. (1994). *Jazz Dance: The Story of American Vernacular Dance.* New York: Da Capo Press. (Original work published 1968.)

Syed, M. (2010). *Bounce: Mozart, Federer, Picasso, Beckham and the Science of Success.* New York: HarperCollins.

Index

Note: The italicized *f* and *t* following page numbers refer to figures and tables, respectively.

A

abdominal curls 94
accents 3-4
Achilles tendonitis 32, 151
aerobic fitness 18-19, 151
affirmations 15-16, 151
African Caribbean jazz dance 143-144, 151
agonist muscles 28, 151
Ailey, Alvin 135, 138
alignment 56, 56*f*, 151
American Bandstand (TV show) 129
anaerobic fitness 18, 151
analyzing movement skills 40-45, 44*t*
anatomy 28, 29*f*. *See also* body alignment
ankles alignment 56
ankle sprain 32, 151
antagonist muscles 28, 151
arch jump 101
arm isolations 84
arm positions 62-69*f*
artistic expression 7
artistic interpretation 54
assemblé 102
Astaire, Fred 131-132
attentive repetition 49, 151
authentic jazz dance 128, 143, 151
axial movement 95, 151

B

ball-and-socket joint 30, 151
ball change 98
ballet 7
basic jazz walk 109
B-boying. *See* breaking
beat 45-46, 46*f*, 151
Beatty, Talley 135, 139
Bennett, Michael 134-135
bent hand position 72*f*
Bethel, Pepsi 5, 136, 151
big apple 128, 151
black bottom 127, 151
body alignment 56-59, 56*f*, 59*f*. *See also* anatomy
body-half connectivity 17, 151
body lotions and powders 27
body positions 72*f*-77*f*
body shape 40-42151
bow position 76*f*

bow stretch 93
breaking 130, 151
breath connectivity 17, 151
Buraczeski, Danny 140
butterfly position 74*f*
butterfly stretch 91

C

Cabin in the Sky 136
cakewalk 103, 126, 151
camel walk 111
cartwheel 121
cat and cow stretch 93
cat position 76*f*
cat walk 111
causal body 80, 151
centering 14-15, 151
center stage 78, 78*f*
cervical spine 58, 151
chaînés 114
Charleston 104, 127, 151
Chicago 134
choreographer's intent 147-148
chug 99
classical arm positions 65*f*-67*f*
classical concert jazz dance 145, 151
classical first position 61*f*
classical hand position 71*f*
classical jazz dance 143, 151
classical second position 62*f*
clip turn 118
clothing 12-13
cobra position 75*f*
cobra stretch 92
coffee grinder 120
Cole, Jack 20, 68*f*, 132-133, 151
combinations 21, 122, 151
commercial hip-hop 144, 151
commercial jazz dance 135, 144, 151
compass turn 115
compression 34, 34*t*, 151
concentric contraction 28, 151
concert jazz dance 141, 145-146, 151
conditioning 21, 152
conditioning techniques, basic 89-94
connected breathing 152
connectivity 41-42, 152

Conte, Lou 140

contemporary commercial jazz dance 145, 152

contemporary concert jazz dance 146

cool-down 22, 152

coordination exercises 20, 152

coordination techniques, basic 87-89

core-distal connectivity 17, 152

core strength 20

counting music 45-46, 46*f*

counting syncopation 47*f*

cow position 77*f*

crazy legs 105

cross lateral connectivity 17-18, 152

cross-training 7

D

dab effort action 44, 44*t*, 45

dance bag 13-14

dégagé 87

De Lavallade, Carmen 139

deliberate practice 47-49, 152

demi plié 81

Denishawn Dance Company 132

diagnosis 34, 34*t*

direct expressiveness 5

directions, studio and stage 77-78, 78*f*

direct space 42, 152

disco 130, 152

downstage 78, 78*f*, 152

drag leap 118

drag step 112

Dunham, Katherine 136, 137-138, 139, 152

duple meter 46*f*

dynamic contraction 28, 152

dynamics 2-3

E

eccentric contraction 28, 152

effort actions 44-45, 44*t*, 152

elevation (for injuries) 34, 34*t*, 152

en croix 88

endurance 18-19, 21, 152

ensemble skills 53-54

equipment 26

even dynamics 3

exercises across the floor 21, 109-122

    floor work and inversions 119-122

    jazz walks and footwork 109-113

    jump, hop, and leap steps 116-119

    turns 114-116

exercises in the center 21, 96-108

    hop, jump, and leap steps and variations 100-103

    step and step variations 96-99

traditional jazz steps 103-106

    turns 107-108

expression 52

F

Faccuito, Eugene Louis (Luigi) 136, 152

fad dances 129, 152

feedback loops 50-51

feel it from inside 49, 152

fifth-position classical arms 67*f*

fifth-position jazz arms 64*f*

first-position classical arms 65*f*

first-position jazz arms 63*f*

fist hand position 70*f*

flat back 82

flat back position 72*f*

flea hop 106

flex hand position 71*f*

flexibility 19, 21, 152

flick effort action 44, 44*t*, 45

flick kick 103

float effort action 44, 44*t*, 45

flocking 53-54, 152

flow 50, 152

flow state 50

flow states 50

focus 43, 152

follow-through 42, 152

foot positions 60*f*-62*f*

forward lunge position 73*f*

forward lunge stretch 90

forward pelvic tilt 58, 152

Fosse, Bob 134

fourth-position classical arms 66*f*

fourth-position jazz arms 64*f*

Fred Astaire turn 114

fusion dance styles 139-140

G

gear, dance 13-14

general space 27, 152

Gennaro, Peter 133

Giordano, Gus 137, 152

glide effort action 44, 44*t*, 45

gliding joint 30, 152

Graham, Martha 139

grand battement 89

grand battement hop 116

grand jeté 118

grand plié 81

grapevine 110

gravity 4-5

gross body 80, 152

H

hand positions 70f-72f
Harris, Rennie 141
head isolations 83
head-tail connectivity 17, 152
health benefits 6-7
health issues. *See safety* and *health issues*
heel stretch 91
hinge 82
hinge joint 30, 152
hinge on knees 119
hinge position 74f
hinge to knees 119
hip-hop 131, 145, 152
hip isolations 85
hips alignment 57-58
history of jazz dance
    Big Band Era 128
    birth of jazz music 127
    current trends 131
    disco and street dance 130
    as entertainment 131-135
    fad dances 129
    Jazz Age 127
    music video era 130
    as a performing art 135-142
    post-World War II 129
    roots of 126
    as social dance 126-131
    Swing Era 128-129
    vaudeville 131
    vogue and hip-hop 130-131
hitch glide 111
hitch kick 117
hop 100
horizontal swing 82
Horton, Lester 138
Humphrey, Doris 132
hydration 35
hyperextension 19, 57, 152
hyperlordosis 58, 59f, 152

I

ice (for injuries) 34, 34t, 152
impact phrasing 3
improvisation 5
impulse phrasing 3
indirect space 42, 153
individual style 5, 20
initiation 40, 153
injuries
    about 31
    ankle pain 32
    knee pain 33

    lower back pain 33
    lower leg pain 32-33
    PRICED 33-34, 34t
inner initiation 40, 153
intonation cues 38, 153
isolations 20-21, 153
isolation techniques, basic 83-86

J

Jack Cole position jazz arms 68f
Jackson, Michael 135
jazz arm positions 62-64f
jazz back fall 121
jazz chassé 109
jazz dance
    benefits of studying 6-7
    class expectations and etiquette 7-8
    class structure 20-22
    clothing expectations 12
    commercial jazz dance styles 144-145
    concert jazz dance styles 145-146
    definitions and aspects of 2-5
    forms and styles 142-146
    gear bag contents 13-14
    history of 126-142
    mental preparation for 14-16
    mind-body preparation 16-18
    musician role 22
    physical preparation 18-20
    roots of 126
    shoes for 13
    as social dance 126-131
    student role 22
    teacher role 22
    theatrical jazz dance styles 143-144
    traditional jazz dance styles 142-143
    viewing etiquette and tips 146-149
jazz funk. *See* street jazz
jazz hand position 70f
jazz run 110
jazz slide 121
jazz square 98
jazz strut 112
jitterbug 128, 142, 153
joint movements 30
joints 28, 30, 153
jump 100
jump apart together 101
jumper's knee 33, 153
jump rhythm technique 140

K

Kelly, Gene 132, 133
Kidd, Michael 133, 134
kimbo 99

kinesiology 30-31, 31*f*, 153
kinesthetic sense 16-17, 153
kinesthetic sensing 51, 153
knee alignment 57

L
lateral 82
lateral plane 30, 31*f*
lateral position 73*f*
leap 102
leg isolations 86
leg lifts 93
Lindy 106, 153
Lindy hop 106, 128, 142
listening 38-39
locking 130, 153
locomotive movement 95, 153
lumbar spine 58, 59*f*, 153
lumbosacral strain 33, 153
lyrical 144, 153

M
mambo 129, 153
marking 49, 153
Mattox, Matt 137, 153
McIntyre, Diane 139
McKayle, Donald 139
mechanical low back pain 33, 153
mental preparation 14-16
mess around 107
Michaels, Mia 141
middle parallel position jazz arms 69*f*
mind-body preparation 16-18
minstrel shows 126, 153
mirror feedback 51
modern concert jazz dance 145-146, 153
Moonwalk (Bob Fosse) 113
Moonwalk (Michael Jackson) 113
movement patterns 17-18
movement technique, learning
    about 38-40
    analyzing movement skills 40-45, 44*t*
    artistic interpretation 54
    attentive repetition 49
    body parts 40
    body shape 40
    connectivity 41-42
    deliberate practice 47-49
    doing 39-40
    effort actions 44-45, 44*t*
    enhancing performance 47-51
    ensemble skills 53-54
    expression 52
    feedback loops 50-51
    feel it from inside 49
    flow states 50
    follow-through 42
    honing musicality and rhythmic skills 45-47, 46*f*, 47*f*
    initiation 40-41
    listening 38-39
    marking 49
    performance attitude 51-54
    sequence 41
    use of space 42-43
    use of time 43
    use of weight 44
    watching 39
muscular system 28, 29*f*
musicality and rhythmic skills, honing 45-47, 46*f*, 47*f*
musical theater jazz dance 143-144, 153
musician role 22
music videos 130

N
Nagrin, Daniel 139
natural hand position 71*f*
neutral foot position 60*f*
novelty fad dances 130, 153
nutrition 35

O
observation skills 38, 153
oppositional accents 3-4
outer initiation 40-41, 153
over the top 118-119

P
paddle turn 108
parallel first position 60*f*
parallel fourth position 61*f*
parallel second position 61*f*
pas de Bourrée 98
pas de Bourrée turn 108
pathway 43, 153
pencil turn 116
percussive movement 3
performance attitude 51-54
personal health information 27-28
personal safety 27-28
personal space 27, 153
Peters, Michael 135
physical fitness benefits 6-7
physical preparation 18-20
pike jump 102
pirouette 115
pivot turn 107
plane 30-31, 31*f*, 153

pony 106
popping 130, 153
positions, basic jazz dance
    arm positions 62-69*f*
    body positions 72*f*-77*f*
    foot positions 60*f*-62*f*
    hand positions 70*f*-72*f*
power 18, 153
preparatory position classical arms 65*f*
preparatory position jazz arms 63*f*
press effort action 44, 44*t*, 45
pretzel stretch 91
PRICED 33-34, 34*t*
primary curves 58, 153
progression 28, 153. *See also* exercises across
    the floor
pronation 56, 56*f*, 153
protection 33-34, 34*t*, 153
punch effort action 44, 44*t*, 45
push-ups 94

Q
quadruple meter 46*f*, 47*f*

R
recalling 15, 153
relevé 81, 83
respect 7-8
rest 34, 34*t*, 35, 153
retiré 88
retiré hop 116
Revelations 138
rhythm 2-4
rhythmic cues 38, 153
rhythmic phrasing 46
rib isolations 85
Rivera, Chita 133
Robbins, Jerome 133
Rome and Jewels 141
rosin 27

S
safety and health issues
    injuries 31-34, 34*t*
    kinesiology 30-31, 31*f*
    muscular system 28, 29*f*
    personal safety 27-28
    skeletal system 28, 29*f*
    studio safety 26-27
sagittal plane 30, 31*f*
saut de chat 118
scissor step 105
scoop position jazz arms 69*f*
scorpion position 76*f*
scorpion stretch 92

S-curve position jazz arms 69*f*
seated first position 75*f*
seated first-position stretch 92
seated second position 75*f*
seated second-position stretch 92
seated side fall 120
secondary curves 58, 153
second-position classical arms 66*f*
second-position jazz arms 63*f*
sequence 41, 154
sequential sequencing 41, 154
shape 42, 154
Shawn, Ted 132
shifting transition 42, 154
shin splints 33, 154
shoes, jazz 13
Shorty George 104
shoulder isolations 84
side fall 120
side lunge descent and ascent 90
side lunge position 73*f*
Siegenfeld, Billy 140
Simonson, Lynn 139, 140-141
simultaneous initiation 41, 154
simultaneous sequence 41, 154
sinking hip 57, 154
sissonne 102
sixth-position jazz arms 67*f*
skeletal system 28, 29*f*
slash effort action 44, 44*t*, 45
sock hop 129, 154
soutenu turn 115
space, use of 42-43
spacing 53, 154
spatial sense 16, 154
spinal alignment 58-59, 59*f*
spiral descent 120
spiral descent and ascent 91
split stretch 93
St. Dennis, Ruth 132
stage left 78, 78*f*, 154
stage right 77-78, 78*f*, 154
stag leap 117
standing contraction position 74*f*
standing contractions 89
step and step variations 96
step together and touch 97
step together step 99
step touch 97
straight jump 101
street jazz 144, 154
strength 18, 21, 154
stretching 14

Stroman, Susan 135
students, role of 22
studio and stage directions 77-78, 78*f*
studio safety 26-27
subtle body 80, 154
successive sequence 41, 154
sugar 104
sundari head isolations 84
supination 56, 56*f*, 154
Susie Q 110
swing 3, 128, 142, 154
syncopation 4, 47, 47*f*, 154

T
teachers, role of 22
techniques, basic jazz dance
    about 79-80
    conditioning techniques 89-94
    coordination techniques 87-89
    isolation techniques 83-86
    warm-up techniques 80-83
tendu 87
tendu soutenu 88
theatrical jazz dance 143-144
third-position classical arms 66*f*
third-position jazz arms 64*f*
thoracic spine 58, 154
three-step turn 107
Thriller 135
time, use of 43
touch 97
touch turn 114-115
traditional jazz dance 142-143, 154
traditional position jazz arms 68*f*

transformational transition 42, 154
transition 42, 154
transverse plane 30-31, 31*f*
triangle position 77*f*
triangle stretch 90
triple meter 46*f*
triple step 112
triplet 110
truckin' 106
tucking under 58, 154
tuck jump 101

U
upper-lower connectivity 17, 154
upstage 78, 78*f*, 154

V
vaudeville 131, 154
Vegas walk 112
Verdon, Gwen 134
vibratory phrasing 3
viewing jazz dance performances 146-149
visualization 15, 154
vocabulary cues 38, 154
vogue 130, 154
V position jazz arms 68*f*

W
warm-up 14-20, 154
warm-up techniques, basic 80-83
Weidman, Charles 132
weight, use of 44
West Side Story 133
World War II 128-129
wring effort action 44, 44*t*, 45

About the Author

James Robey, MFA, is assistant professor of dance and department chair at Webster University in St. Louis, Missouri, where he received the Messing Faculty Award in 2015. He was director of the prestigious Ridgefield Conservatory of Dance for 10 years, during which he also created the Robey Jazz Dance Technique and Syllabus. He has taught as faculty or adjunct faculty at numerous universities, schools for the performing arts, and dance studios.

Robey was artistic director and company artist for James Robey Dance for 14 years. He has danced for many companies, beginning his dance career in 1990. He has also acted as choreographer for numerous ballets and dance ensembles over the years, and he has presented at conferences and written numerous articles on jazz dance and related topics.

Robey is on the board of directors of the American College Dance Association and is a member of the National Dance Education Organization, National Association of Schools of Dance, and Phi Kappa Phi Honor Society.

Perfect introductory guides for learning, performing, and viewing dance genres!

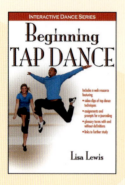

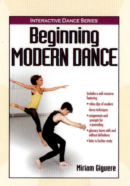

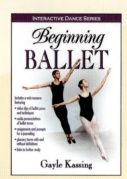

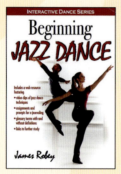

Human Kinetics' Interactive Dance Series includes resources for modern dance, ballet, tap dance, jazz dance, and musical theatre dance that support introductory dance technique courses taught through dance, physical education, and fine arts departments. Each student-friendly text includes a web resource offering video clips of dance instruction, learning aides, assignments, and activities. The Interactive Dance Series offers students a guide to learning, performing, and viewing dance.

Contact your sales representative today for an exam copy!
HumanKinetics.com/SalesRepresentatives

HUMAN KINETICS
The Information Leader in Physical Activity & Health